1

Contents

Introduction

Brian: Look, you've got it all wrong! You don't need to follow me, you don't need to follow anybody! You've got to think for yourselves! You're all individuals!

Crowd: Yes! We're all individuals!

Brian: You're all different!

Crowd: Yes! We are all different!

Man in crowd: I'm not.

Crowd: Shhhh.

From *Monty Python's The Life of Brian* (1979, dir. Terry Jones, script by Graham Chapman, John Clease, Terry Gilliam, Eric Idle, Terry Jones and Michael Palin).

There are two ways of viewing the role of a teacher. One is to see him/her as a technician who needs to demonstrate competence in a number of

3

'skills' – lesson planning, classroom management and so on. In this view, he needs to leave his personal values outside of his workplace and perform his role with the utmost objectivity. In the second view, the teacher's personal values are, for better or for worse, at the very heart of her work, the very tools with which she forges her personal style, and without which she is lost. To deny this, so the argument goes, is to cease to be a human being and to become instead a robot, and learners are not going to relate very well to a robot.

My own journey through a teaching career has brought me further and further towards the view that the teacher's personal values, along with his character and personality, really do matter. Of course, if we go along with this idea, we run into the problem of formal hierarchy; what happens when a teacher's values clash with those of his employer, or with those who have the authority to judge him, or with the mainstream culture? Such a situation, when it arises, presents the teacher with a dilemma – should she fight, take flight or simply play dead? Is it ever justified for teachers to challenge authority in defence not just of material terms and conditions but of fundamental values? If so, is it possible to do this successfully?

Throughout my teaching career, I have tended to view myself as a sort of *anarchist*. In the sense that I am using it, the word *anarchism* simply denotes the belief that, since social institutions, the education system included, tend to function in such a way as to restrict individual creativity and stifle the development of human potential, they need to be dismantled and rebuilt from the bottom up. This can be achieved non-violently, and, in the case of education, the people best placed to take a lead in the project are teachers. Furthermore, an anarchist might argue, once the education system has been thus reconstructed, it will function so as to equip those passing through it with the ability to dismantle and rebuild other social institutions, for example the family, the community or the political system. But we are getting ahead of ourselves. Before we can consider the idea of using education as a tool for social, economic and political transformation we need to understand education itself and its role in guiding and moulding the development of the individual.

All of us need to develop in infancy the ability to engage with our environment in such a way that we understand it and feel intimately involved with it (see Piaget, 1936). When this starts to happen to an individual, she acquires too basic strategies; she learns *both* to adapt her own behaviour to accommodate the realities of her environment *and* to change her environment to accommodate her needs. As her mind develops, the environment she perceives around her expands to encompass not just her immediate physical surroundings but the network of relationships she needs to forge and maintain, the culture she's been born into and, ultimately, the social, economic and political realities she has to contend with. If she has benefitted from a good education, that is one which has given her every opportunity to realise her full potential, she will be equipped to deal with these higher level realities not just by adapting her behaviour to accommodate them, but by trying to change them. This, in short, is why education and politics are two sides of the same coin, and why we can say that education is the continuation of politics by other means.

In the 1950s, the psychiatrist Humphry Osmond coined the word *psychedelic* to describe the kinds of visionary experiences accessible through the use of hallucinogenic drugs – experiences he believed to be manifestations of an expanded consciousness. However, I like to use the word in the broader, non-pharmaceutical sense of finding joy, wonder and the opportunity for personal transformation in all of life's experiences, and I believe that this is what education, at its best, can achieve.

I also want the word to signify a breaking through of surface perceptions to find deeper truths, whether philosophical, psychological, social or political, a cleansing of the 'doors of perception' by means other than drugs, not just for learners but for teachers too. The underlying proposition here is that, if we can alter *consciousness*, our own and that of others, we can change society. I daresay a great many teachers would agree with me here in principle, but the reality for lots of people going through the education system is that it is a soul-destroying daily grind of an experience, to be endured for the sake of some future extrinsic reward, not unlike a prison sentence. It is likely to leave its victims with lifelong inferiority complexes to deal with. Teachers might argue that they are powerless to change the system, but I think that such an attitude is over-pessimistic. In so far as teachers are culpable, it is in the tendency that so many of them have to be unreflective, and to think of themselves as *apolitical*, blank sheets onto which the system can imprint itself.

I think that teachers have a lot more power to change things than they realise, and that they should think in terms of trying to change the system from within. Admittedly, this will not be an easy task as there are serious obstacles that would need to be overcome. One such is the fact that society's elites, the opinion-formers and policy-makers on educational matters, tend grossly disproportionately to have been educated privately. The problem with this state of affairs is that the aforementioned elites are inevitably afflicted by an unconscious bias towards viewing state education as inferior to private education. Their powers of reason, thus clouded by this delusion, tend to lead them to the conclusion that the performance of the system can, and should, be improved through the application of central government coercion in the form of a prescriptive and punitive inspection regime. It is a narrative that portrays teachers in state education as basically incompetent and untrustworthy when left to their own devices, the 'enemy within'.

Another obstacle is the fact that teachers working in the state sector, though they may well be products themselves of state education, tend to be recruited almost exclusively from the ranks of those who enjoyed school and did very well out of it. Without doubt, most of these people are professional, sincere and hard-working, and they genuinely want their learners to succeed. The trouble is that they tend to struggle to properly understand and empathise with those who do not enjoy school, viewing them as *problems*, deviants who need to be cured of their misguided attitudes and hammered into conformity, or mediocrities of whom little can be expected. What teachers who think like this fail to realise is that, by knocking the nonconformity out of these people, they are also knocking the individuality and creativity out of them, and quite possibly inducing mental health problems in the process. To try to deal with the awkward ones by lowering standards and expectations so that they are given the illusion of success is just as much a betrayal. Some sort of revolution is gravely needed if we are to have a system that works for everyone. And we need a sense of urgency; the problems afflicting the world, especially the environmental emergency, are with us now and we need to start developing generations of people who can stop being part of the problem and start becoming part of the solution.

In the U.K., we have high performing elites in many fields of human endeavour: science & technology, business, culture and sport to name but a few. This is something we are rightly proud of, but this success at the top end tends unfortunately to mask the fact that, beneath the surface, too much of our population is under-educated, having been let down by the education system, and consequently under-productive and under-rewarded. This underlying reality serves to maintain patterns of economic inequality and needs to be challenged. Again, those best positioned to do this are teachers. We need to nail our colours to the mast and take the fight to the enemy, those who want things to go on being as they are, and the way we can do that is by telling a different kind of story about education.

Commentators on education often talk about 'myths' and the need to dispel them so as to make way for 'facts'. They will talk about the need for practice to be evidence-led. It should indeed be evidence-led, but I sometimes detect an insinuation that 'evidence-led' for them means mimicking the methods of the hard sciences by being ultra-focused on collecting quantitative data. Such an attitude is foolish because the study of education is as much about philosophy as it is about science and it ought to value the kinds of insights that can be acquired by experiencing the system subjectively from within. It sometimes seems as if the real intention of those who want to disparage such insight is to put those who disagree with them in their place. To be clear, I am not making the case here for relativism, for the view that all opinions are equally valid. What I am saying is that all opinions *grounded in experience* are valid to some degree, and that their validity increases with the length, variety and the directness of the experience. Empirical evidence matters, but we should not diminish the value of the evidence gathered by teachers themselves day-in-day-out in their classrooms. Teachers need to take their own experiences seriously, to reflect upon them, interpret them, weave stories from them.

In the hard sciences, knowledge may progress by disproving falsehoods experimentally, but in the social sciences, and the study of education is a social science, growth in understanding proceeds through a dialectical process; opposing ideas are discussed and debated and what ultimately emerges is a synthesis of different ideas. And this is not a process that should only take place in lofty academic circles, or amongst policy-makers at the top of the hierarchy, but in staff-rooms and student common-rooms up and down the land, as well as in social media, the mass media and in culture and the arts.

The only myth I want to explode is the myth that it is a good thing to explode myths. Myth is just another word for story. We understand the world and our place in it through stories, of which there are two kinds. On the one hand, there are the insider stories, those developed and distributed by the privileged elites in order to establish the 'truth' of their world view. On the other, there are the outsider stories, these being the ones that struggle to be heard above the noise. In truth, though, neither kind of story is any 'truer' than the other, and the voice of the outsider, if it struggles long enough and hard enough, will be heard.

We are all familiar with the insider story about education. It asserts that teaching is all about being in control. It is held to be self-evident that teachers need to dominate learners and instil respect. A teacher needs to be supremely confident and devoid of self-doubt, and she need to be able to exude this through her very presence. She needs, in short, to be an authoritarian extravert. I simply do not believe that this is all there is to teaching. I think that there is a valid counter-narrative that needs to be told and I want to tell it.

I want to say something about how the book came about. Close to the beginning of my teaching career, whilst working in a secondary school in Central America, I underwent something of a professional crisis. I was trying incredibly hard to apply the methods I'd learned in my teacher training back in the U.K., but was getting nowhere with my students. Not to put too fine a point on it, they hated me and wouldn't do anything I asked them to do. I tried to copy what the other teachers in the school were doing by relating to the learners in a colder, more punitive manner, but this just made matters worse as it gave them a rational justification for hating me. Because I couldn't think of what else to do, I started to write my thoughts down in a journal. The more I wrote, the more I began to weave thoughts together until what emerged was what I can only describe as a rudimentary personal philosophy about teaching based around the idea that empathy should replace authoritarianism as the defining feature of the teacher-student relationship. This new approach didn't work straight away, but I persevered and began to perceive that I was becoming more successful. I used the journal as a way of recording my experiments, rather like a researcher might. It gave me an escape route from the labyrinth I had become lost in. I decided to carry on writing, even after the initial crisis had been overcome, and I kept the writing habit going when I returned to the U.K. and did other things in my career, including working for twelve years in prison education and teaching people to drive..

When writing down my reflections, I often felt more like a journalist doing research into education, or perhaps a film director making a documentary about it, than someone who was an integral part of it. This was difficult in one way because it meant I was never totally at one with my colleagues, always one step removed from the workplace culture, but it was useful in another because it enabled me to look at the workplace with an outsider's eyes and ask the types of 'why' questions that didn't seem to occur to other teachers.

After around 20 years of keeping the journal, it dawned on me that I had enough material for a book and decided to give it a go. The problem I faced was that I had a huge amount of content that needed to be moulded into a structure and this meant making decisions about what to keep and what to throw away. It was like trying to complete a 50,000 piece jigsaw puzzle starting out with 100,000 pieces. I needed to somehow work out which pieces were going to be part of the final picture and which weren't, and I didn't even know what the final picture was going to look like at that stage. Once I had discarded all the irrelevant bits, I still had the job of fitting all the remaining pieces together in the correct order, very much a process of trial-and-error.

Before I could even begin the process of linking together my collection of random thoughts about education into a book, I needed to ask myself what sort of book I wanted it to be. Did I want to write a technical manual for teachers, a book crammed full of teaching methods and lesson ideas? The answer was 'no' because there are lots of books like that already in existence and, in any case, I had by that stage rejected the idea that teaching was essentially about the mastery of a set of technical skills. Did I want the book to be some sort of Marxist rant against the establishment? The answer was again 'no' because, although there was much politics in my journal, some of it very radical, I wanted to write a book that was positive and constructive, that offered pathways by which ordinary teachers could improve education from the bottom up by changing the culture bit by bit, non-aggressively. I suppose I wanted to write the sort of textbook I'd wish I'd had at the start of my teaching career, something that was accessible while at the same time treating readers like intelligent adults. Although the book is firmly grounded in my personal experience, in endeavouring to produce something worthy of publication I have sought to back up my insights with references to secondary sources, both in the educational studies literature and more widely, delving into areas of psychology and cultural studies. I think that what eventually evolved was a book that presented a highly radical vision of what education could be and what teachers could achieve, but one which was grounded in reality and the art of the possible.

I have always been interested in creative writing and this book, in a sense, is just that – a piece of creative writing. What I mean by that is that it has almost felt like what was being written has had a will of its own, pulling me in directions it was never my original intention to go in. It has been a collaboration between the conscious and unconscious parts of my mind and I believe it is all the richer for this.

Slowly but surely, the book began to take shape, but it was still missing something and that something was a single unifying theme. The solution came to me one day when I was reflecting back on my time as a union rep in prison education. When I was performing that role, I became preoccupied with the question of workplace culture and how to change it. The received wisdom on workplace culture states that a good leader might be able to turn around a negative workplace *atmosphere*, but that the underlying *culture* was impossible to change. This is because the behaviour patterns are just too deeply ingrained. But I never accepted this; if individuals can change, why not a culture? The question was how? There was no easy answer; anyone trying to change a culture runs up against the same self-defeating paradox – that the culture is the thing that most of the people operating inside it most treasure, so they will fight with knives, razor blades and broken bottles to protect it. After deep reflection, the answer came to me: *the way to change a culture is to create a counterculture.* Then I started to think about the word 'counterculture' itself. For me, it evoked images of the 1960s – hippies, psychedelia, student protests. In the specifically British context, it meant The Beatles, Swinging London and the satire boom. But then I started to think about the extent to which the sixties counterculture in Britain, fantastic as it was, had been dominated by well-educated middle-class males. The working class, particularly the ones who had been to a 'secondary modern', the inferior of the two types of state secondary school, were largely excluded. Could this explain why the counterculture eventually burnt itself out and was eclipsed in the 1970s and '80s by a conservative backlash, one which *did* encompass working class people? If so, the lesson we might take from this is that any future attempt to resurrect the spirit of the '60s for the present age must, to be more sustainable than the original, involve much greater numbers of people and a much wider socioeconomic spectrum? If we go along with this idea, it is difficult to see how a new counterculture might be born without the movement making inroads into the state education system. This, then, became my unifying theme: counterculture as a concept is both the key to changing the education system from within and the wider social and cultural movement for change to which a reformed education system helps gives birth.

The book puts the case for an approach to education that is learner-centred but practitioner-led. What I mean by 'learner-centred' is that learners are viewed as active partners in a creative process, as opposed to consumers of a product. I see the term 'practitioner-led' as being the antithesis of organisation-led, so it is by definition subversive. The fuller implications of this will, I hope, become clear as the book progresses, but suffice to say for now that I believe that the combination of learner-centredness and practitioner leadership is the key to what you might call 'making a difference'.

In so far as my teaching career has been based on a personal philosophy, such a philosophy stems from the belief that all human beings have within them a potential, but it that is by no means inevitable that such potential comes to fruition. It is prevented from doing so in two ways: either the individual herself fears the potential and represses it, or the wider culture feels threatened by it and oppresses the individual. Of course, both types of barrier mechanism can operate simultaneously and reinforce one another. Since education is concerned with the development of human potential, it must address both mechanisms, but since both of them operate largely at an unconscious level, the role of the teacher is to raise consciousness.

The prelude to my interest in teaching was my interest in psychotherapy. For a while, I imagined that I might do this for a living. I became aware that one way of classifying psychotherapists was to divide them into those who believe that it was the release of emotion that really mattered in the therapeutic process, and those who believe that cognitive self-insight was the key. I allied myself strongly to the latter group and became convinced that therapy was largely a process of learning and understanding. Thus, I became interested in cognitive development and that is what led me, ultimately, to teaching. My personal philosophy of teaching is thus one which very much takes psychotherapy as its template.

I enjoy metaphors and allegories. When I was a child, I used to love the Hans Christian Andersen story about *The Emperor's New Clothes*. In it, a vain Emperor is tricked into believing he is wearing a fine suit of new clothes when he is in fact completely naked. The sycophants around him confirm the lie by complimenting him on his exquisite outfit. And who can blame them? No-one wants to upset the Emperor and risk getting their head chopped off. But what if everyone behaved like that all the time? Falsehoods would never get challenged, truths would never be revealed and nothing would ever improve. A recurring theme of my working life has been a willingness to say from time to time, *"But the Emperor's not wearing any clothes!"*, and to live with consequences. This book is, in many ways, a continuation of that tendency.

When it comes to my view of the human mind, I have always tended to recoil from those theories of education which view the learner as a sort of lab rat, responding in predictable ways to various stimuli. When I look within myself, what I see is a thinking being, self-aware and capable of reflection. I see an individual able to come to independent judgements and of formulating independent opinions. I see a person with an imagination who can create stories which help him to make sense of himself and the world around him. This person has values and opinions. He may respond to stimuli but he is also capable, with the benefit of education, of consciously resisting the impulse to do so. This makes him unpredictable and therefore difficult to manipulate.

So, who is the book actually for? Well, it is for teachers, those in teacher training, those thinking of becoming teachers, and anyone with an interest in education. One of the things I am trying to do is challenge the view that only a certain type of person can be a teacher. I believe that many different types of people have the potential to become great educators. What really matters is that teachers give serious thought to who they are deep within themselves and to what they actually believe. Without such contemplation, the danger is that the teacher, when faced with difficulty, will simply succumb to the culture around her and copy what everyone else is doing, thereby becoming part of the problem.

Although they are welcome to read it, this book is not particularly aimed at politicians, policy-makers, or senior administrators. In so far as I do discuss management, I do so from the perspective of the person being managed rather than the manager. It is probably fair to say that I regard management as an over-rated skill, not strictly necessary, and often counter-productive. No, the book is defiantly and unashamedly about what teachers can do for themselves and aims to encourage them to rise to the challenge of leadership. All too often, places of education are staffed by individuals who have fallen into the mindset of *"If only my managers would do this"*, or *"If only the government would do that"*, thus soldiering on to the ends of their careers with an attitude of wistful pessimism. This book says that, far from being slaves in a system they didn't create, teachers are the ones with the real power and it is they who hold the key to progress.

I am willing to bet that some of the views expressed in the book will seem to some readers to be counter-intuitive, even downright ludicrous, but I make no apology for saying things that I sincerely feel to be true. Anyone in the habit of reflecting deeply about topics that are important to them will be familiar with the phenomenon of the sudden 'aha!' moment, where what was once confusing and incomprehensible becomes in an instant as clear as day. When this happens, the question arises as to whether the thought is a genuine revelation of truth (what we might call an epiphany), or a fantasy concocted by the unconscious mind in order to *obscure* the truth (what we would probably call a delusion). We have no reliable means of telling the two experiences apart and all we can really do is share our thoughts with others so that they decide for themselves how plausible they are. I am as vulnerable to self-deception as anyone else, but the book is ultimately just a story told from one person's perspective. If its themes ring true with some readers, that would be most gratifying. Equally, if it inspires others to develop critiques and counter-arguments, that's okay too.

Chapter 1

Understanding Learning

It is impossible to escape two basic facts about learning. The first is that learning is a transition from dependence to independence that involves struggle, and the second is that no-one can be forced to learn against their will. We could almost call these the fundamental laws of education.

The *first* law implies that, notwithstanding the fact that all educational institutions have a duty of care towards their learners, education and care are, in reality, very different things. Teaching is sometimes included in that family of occupations known as 'the caring professions', but the truth is that educators and people who care for a living tend to have very different impulses when they are in the presence of someone who is struggling. To put it bluntly, if a nurse sees someone struggling, her conditioned reflex is to help them, but a true educator's response should be to let them struggle; the educator's brain is telling her that struggle equals learning and that it would be ethically abhorrent to deny the person the opportunity to learn. This is why teaching is *mostly* about standing back and doing nothing. Or, to put it more generously, it is about watching people struggle and trying to resist the temptation to help them for as long as possible. This would not work on an intensive care ward.

Another way of phrasing the *second* law is to say that learning and the motivation to learn cannot be separated. This makes learning very different from, say, having a haircut. In the haircut scenario, things are of course much easier all round if the child wants the haircut and co-operates willingly with those trying to give him one. However, in the hypothetical scenario of his being unwilling to co-operate, this would not necessarily mean that the haircut could not take place because he could in theory simply be strapped to a chair such that resistance was futile, with a gag in his mouth to prevent him biting or spitting. Then, an assistant could hold his head still while the barber went about his business. In the case of cutting a child's hair, then, motivation on the part of the child is desirable but not essential. With learning, by contrast, motivation is absolutely essential. Admittedly, this is simply a statement of the obvious but, to hear some commentators speak, you would think that if it were only possible to restrain someone so thoroughly that they were physically incapable of averting their gaze, rather like the character Alex in Stanley Kubrick's film *A Clockwork Orange* (1971), and force them to pay attention to whatever it was you wanted them to learn, this would prove a successful strategy and the person subject to it would one day be grateful. In truth, you can control someone's body if you are more powerful than them, but you cannot control their mind without their consent.

Forcing a child to confirm to the outward behavioural conventions of learning in circumstances when the child doesn't want to learn what it has been ordained he should learn is a type of abuse. It is ironic that, when it comes to sex, we have a legal age of consent based on the premise that a child is incapable of giving it, but when it comes to formal education this principle is reversed and the child is assumed to be incapable of *withholding* consent. Mercifully, the blatant use of physical force is no longer deemed an acceptable practice in education. It has been replaced by more psychological forms of coercion, more humane but equally as futile.

The word 'learning' is thrown around liberally in all sorts of contexts but what exactly is it? A superficial consideration of this question might conclude that it can be defined as a change in a person's behaviour over time. This is understandable because behaviour is something that can be observed, and if you can observe something you can measure and record it. Thinking about learning in this way allows a structuring of the learning process such that the teacher records the learner's behaviour both before and after the lesson and the difference between the two constitutes learning. This approach is attractive to researchers, managers and evaluators because such people like things that can be measured and recorded.

Conceptualising learning as a series of adjustments in observable behaviour over time can be useful up to a point, but it cannot be the whole of what learning is about, at least not for human beings. It is just too limited, ignoring as it does cognitive phenomena that are not directly observable or measurable, examples being *consciousness, understanding* and *creativity*. If we base formal education wholly on the behavioural approach, we will produce individuals who are great at following rules, but who have no understanding of why the rules work, and who are clueless over what to do when the rules don't work and new ones have to be improvised.

When I was in my teens, there was a craze for something called the *Rubik's Cube*, a 3-D geometry puzzle in the shape of a cube whose surfaces could be moved in relation to one another. Each surface was composed of nine coloured squares and the aim was to manipulate the cube in such a way that you ended up with each surface being composed of squares of one uniform colour. There was enormous kudos to be had amongst one's peers for being able to solve the puzzle. I acquired such a cube and began to experiment with different ways of manipulating its surfaces. The more I experimented, the more my understanding of how to manoeuvre the particular parts of the cube to where I wanted them to be grew. Eventually, I managed to get to the point where I had the puzzle around two-thirds completed. Then I began to get frustrated with myself for not being quite able to finish and I got hold of an instruction manual for how to complete the puzzle. This was simply a set of step-by-step instructions, what we might call an algorithm. I duly followed the instructions and completed the puzzle. I was pleased at first, but quickly started to feel angry with myself for not having persevered with the independent approach where I was learning by using my innate problem-solving capacity – my *creativity*. I felt something of a fraud. To have persisted with this approach would have taken a long time, more time than I realistically was prepared to devote, as well as enormous self-discipline and patience. Suppose, however, that I had been guided by a teacher and that this teacher, rather than simply telling me how to complete the puzzle, had thrown in little interventions along the lines of, *"Have you thought about doing ….. ?"*, or *"What do you think might happen if you ….. ?"*. The teacher would have been encouraging me to use my own creativity whilst at the same time providing a supportive framework, an approach known as 'scaffolding'. In my opinion, one year of education in which the learner is taught like this is worth ten years of education where he is being conditioned to blindly conform to pre-determined sequences of observable behaviours.

The need for teachers to promote creativity may seem obvious to us now, but in the early years of the 20th century the view that learning was about moulding behaviour was very much the orthodox one, particularly when it came to the working classes and the state provision of education. It is tempting to speculate that those who held this view may have been influenced by the industrial assembly line method where processes were broken down into simple tasks and workers trained to perform them like automatons. Dewey (1916), however, went against the grain on this by arguing that natural learning entailed social interaction and environmental exploration, with the teacher acting as facilitator/guide rather than instructor. These ideas were later picked up on by Piaget (1936, op. cit.), Vygotsky (1930-1934/1978), and Bruner (1960); Piaget emphasised exploration of the physical environment, while Vygotsky and Bruner paid more attention to the ways in which learners interacted with their social and cultural environments. Bruner in particular put story-telling at the heart of the learning process.

Perhaps one way of settling the debate between those who believe in training people to follow set behaviour patterns and those who want to promote creativity would be to draw the distinction between *surface* learning and *deep* learning and to argue that both are useful in their own ways. If we take as an example the cultural phenomenon known as 'political correctness', we can see that it is perfectly possible for someone to learn to say 'person of colour' instead of 'coloured', or 'disabled' instead of 'handicapped'. A trainer simply rewards them with approval when they say the correct word and withholds the reward when they say the incorrect one. Someone who has shown this change in behaviour has, in some sense, become 'educated'. It is clear that if this person then progressed from this simple behavioural change onto developing an understanding of *why* it is better to use one term rather than another they could be said to have become educated in a deeper sense. But, if we are unable to achieve the deeper form of learning in the mass of the population, we might take consolation in the knowledge that the simpler variety is better than nothing as it will prevent the inadvertent giving of offence.

To use another example, I have heard people with severe learning difficulties 'read' in the sense that they have learnt to phonetically decode the symbols on a page, but that does not mean that can they read in the sense of being able to extract meaning from written texts. One could argue that teaching them to phonetically decode is pointless because it is of no practical use to them. On the other hand, if a learner gets pleasure from believing that she can read, maybe it is not such a bad thing.

In general, the defence of superficial learning is four-fold:

- Not everyone has the *innate capacity* to be educated in the deeper sense.

- Not everyone has the *desire* to be educated in the deeper sense.

- Some are not yet *ready* to be educated in the deeper sense.

- Society has no *need* for everyone to be educated in the deeper sense.

It is for you, the readers, to decide for yourselves whether these are valid defences or simply lame excuses, but I would ask you to reserve judgement until after you have read the next chapter.

Chapter 2

The Creative Learner

As we saw in the previous chapter, creativity is the ability of an individual to access and utilise her innate capacity for inventing original solutions to problems, as opposed to relying on pre-formulated methods passed on to them. It is clearly an extremely valuable quality to possess and most would agree that it is something the education system ought to be trying to promote, but Robinson and Aronica (2016) argue that schooling, as it is presently organised, actually *destroys* a child's natural creativity. The reason for this, they believe, is that we are still living with the legacy of pre-Deweyan thinking. They point out that, when state education systems first began to become established in industrialised countries, from the mid-19th century onwards, schools were organised along factory lines, with emphasis on obedience to authority and the satisfactory performance of standardised tasks. This undoubtedly made sense when the reality for most working class children was that they would, on reaching adulthood, go into manual jobs requiring little or no capacity for creativity, but what about the world we're living in now? Although assembly line production persists in manufacturing industry to this day, the system is no longer the norm for most workers. The modern economy is marked by rapid change and unpredictability and, to thrive in this environment, a worker needs to respond to problems creatively, as opposed to following a standardised routine, or simply waiting for the boss to tell him what to do.

Apart from the economic consequences of not educating people to think for themselves, another worry is that it leads to large numbers of people falling prey to those who tell them what they want to hear, what they want to hear chiefly being that their problems and anxieties are not their fault but the fault of others, whether the others in question are economic migrants, ethnic minorities or what are described as 'the elites'. Without a developed capacity for critical thinking, all it takes for people to be manipulated en masse is for an unscrupulous demagogue to tap into their deep-seated anger and give it direction. People are better than that, potentially, but if we want to try to alter this state of affairs, we need to understand something about why it exists.

Before we are even born, from the moment our brains are capable of it, we begin accumulating experiences. These experiences allow us to construct 'mental maps', or 'personal constructs' (Kelly, 1955) – our own personal theories about how the world operates – which we then carry around with us in our heads. The more experiences we accumulate, the more accurate these theories become. We are, in other words, innately capable of working things out for ourselves without being told what to think. The trouble is that, once we have accumulated enough of these mental maps to get by in life, we are in danger of resting on our laurels and of no longer creating new ones. This is okay when we only ever have to deal with familiar situations, but the old mental maps become a hindrance when we are confronted with new challenges. When this happens, we don't really know what to do. We will perhaps keep faith with our old mental maps in the belief that they'll come good for us, or submit to the authority of someone who claims to have the answers. We would avoid these pitfalls, however, if only we could somehow train ourselves to me more comfortable with letting go of the pre-existing mental maps and making completely new ones out of the information before us.

At the start of the coronavirus crisis in 2020, there were calls from politicians for people to use their 'common sense' in relation to social distancing. But then a great many of the people themselves began to complain about lack of clarity and guidance, and to demand a set of rules to follow. Conditioned by factory-style schooling to follow instructions and obey authority, they could not cope with being put in a situation where they had to think for themselves. Then there was another set of people who responded to the situation by behaving as if it were a national holiday, i.e. they fell back on a pre-existing mental map.

If we define 'common sense' as a set of understandings that people are just born with and can therefore invoke at will, expressing disapproval over its absence is pointless because it just doesn't exist. What led me to this conclusion was the experience of spending endless hours sitting alongside novice drivers trying to stop them crashing into things. What *does* exist in the human mind is the capacity, in response to new challenges, to over time create new mental maps, new ways of understanding, as an alternative to falling back on old ones. We ought to be able to do this quite naturally, and I think that young children can do it without even trying, but most people have their capacity to be creative in this way damaged by their experiences of schooling. Rather than systematically destroying creativity, teachers should be nurturing it. The question is, *"How do you nurture creativity?"* Let's look at a range of different theoretical traditions and how each in turn might answer that question.

The behaviourist tradition, as expounded in the work, for example, of BF Skinner (1938), sees education as the systematic conditioning of learners to respond to stimuli. It has, I think, little to offer us in our search for an understanding of how to foster creativity since it is concerned only with what can be observed. Creativity cannot be observed, at least not directly, because it is an internal psychological process; a person can be creative without actually *doing* anything at all.

Perhaps a more fruitful avenue to follow would start with Pinker's (1999) theory that the human mind is essentially an information processing machine – a biological computer which evolved to help us cope with the kinds of threats encountered by our hunter gatherer ancestors. As such, it is not necessarily well-equipped for dealing with the sorts of threats presented by the modern world. Consider, for example, the driving of motor vehicles; we are initially hampered in our attempts to do this safely by such impediments as inaccurate attempts at risk assessment, an insufficient concentration span, and the intrusion of aggressive impulses when we feel threatened. These impediments arise from the fact that our brains evolved to help us survive in a very different environment. However, to compensate for this problem, we have evolved something called *learning*. Every time we make a mistake, we make a mental record of it and reflect on it so that, over a period of time, the frequency of our mistakes diminishes. Our brains have taken in information, processed it and produced adaptations in response. Here we see the beginnings of creativity.

The ability to learn in this way evolved tens of millennia ago when we got bigger, more powerful brains. We upgraded our computers, so to speak. This allowed us to survive in different environments and even to transform our environment to suit our survival needs. The development of this capacity is connected to the evolution of *language*; this allowed ideas to be developed collaboratively and shared, as well as to be mused over in solitary contemplation so that they could be refined and perfected. We're still capable of this now, but it only takes place if there is evolutionary pressure for it to take place, if it is a question of adapt or become extinct, or at least adapt or endure hardship. Thus, when the environment remains stable, it is sufficient for tried and tested ideas to be simply handed down through the generations, but a changing environment demands creativity.

One practical approach to teaching which makes explicit use of the conceptualisation of the mind as a computer is 'neurolinguistic programming' (NLP). Developed by Andreas, Bandler and Grinder (1979), its basic assumption is that, if various techniques can be mastered, the mind can be 're-programmed' to function more effectively. Here are five examples of NLP techniques:

In the technique known as 'modelling', the subject wishing to develop a particular skill or personal attribute identifies another person whom they would like to emulate, observes them closely, and copies their behaviour in as much detail as possible.

In the technique known as 'anchoring', the subject links a particular mental image to a particular feeling and thus becomes able to conjure up said feeling at will by invoking the image.

In the technique known as 're-framing', negative experiences are re-interpreted in such a way as to emphasise the positive aspects of the situation.

The technique known as 'mirroring' takes advantage of the fact that human beings tend to be unconsciously attracted to people they believe are similar to them. The subject copies the other person's body language, thus giving the other person's unconscious mind the message that they are similar to them.

In the technique known as 'dissociation', the subject deals with unpleasant feelings or bad memories by imaginatively removing himself from his own body and observing himself from a distance.

The idea that the mind can be 're-programmed' offers some hope that it can be freed from the influence of old mental maps and as a result become more creative, but is this hope real or illusory? Are we perhaps at risk of confusing a useful, if limited, analogy with literal reality? Astonishing advancements in artificial intelligence have meant that we now have machines capable of mimicking, even improving on, human thought processes. Such technology promises to be very useful, but is there a danger of it influencing our understanding of *human* intelligence to such a degree that we begin to lose sight of the fact that the human mind is not *really* a machine? The consequence of this fallacy – that the human mind is literally a computer – for education is that teachers might start to regard learners as programmable machines and think only in terms of working out how to programme them. What is lost here is any acknowledgment of the fact that the human mind has the capacity not only to process data, but also to think conscious thoughts and make conscious plans, as well as to feel emotions, and out of all this construct *stories* which communicate *meaning*. Pinker's comparison of the mind to a computer, then, has much promise but also the potential to lead us down blind alleys.

One obvious difference between the mind and a computer is that, unlike a computer, a human learner needs to feel a buzz of excitement as she works towards her goal and to get a fix of euphoria when she experiences the *eureka!* moment. If these things are absent, creativity is absent, and she might as well just go through the motions and draw on her old mental maps to get her through the drudgery.

Another important emotional factor, this time working *against* creativity, is anxiety – the feeling that something bad may be about to happen. When a person feels anxious, he experiences the situation he is in as threatening and wants to either fight it or flee from it; learning from it is the last thing on his mind. If, on the other hand, he starts to feel less anxious, he allows himself to develop a sense of wonder in his situation and wants to explore its possibilities, perceiving it as a toy to be played with.

'The Yerkes-Dodson Law', or 'Goldilocks Theory' (1908), states that there is an optimal level of arousal in learning. Too little, and the learner will be too bored to learn. Too much, and he will be too anxious to learn. But just the right amount will make her curious and motivated. This is not an issue for AI machines!

The *humanist* perspective on learning is radically different to both behaviourism and the information processing model in that it puts the subjective emotional experience of the learner at the very heart of learning. A key figure in humanist psychology was the psychotherapist Carl Rogers (1961), who argued that a successful *therapeutic* relationship was one in which defensive psychological barriers were dismantled and the client could start to express her true self as opposed to an unrealistic, idealised self. I was aware of Rogers' ideas before I became a teacher and took them as illicit contraband through the door marked 'teaching career' with me. Through the years, I have become more and more convinced that Rogers' concept of the therapeutic relationship is as applicable in teaching as it is in psychotherapy and that the primary goal of a teacher should be to achieve the lowering of defensive barriers on both sides of the teacher-learner relationship. The more the teacher can do this, the less anxious learners will feel about showing their vulnerabilities and the more relaxed they'll feel about taking risks.

Getting to the point where everyone feels emotionally secure enough to do this is not easy, but in Rogers' approach one achieves this by embodying three essential qualities: *empathy* (understanding what it feels like to be the other person and communicating this understanding to them), *genuineness* (being honest about one's own feelings so that one is not in any way being manipulative by faking one's responses), and *acceptance* (not making moral judgements about the other person). If we define *faith* as the feeling of certainty that things will ultimately turn out all right despite the absence of evidence to suggest that this will be the case, then for a learner to open himself up to the transformative power of education is a leap of faith – faith in the teacher, faith in the process, and faith in his own potential. This is what teachers are trying to achieve when they use the humanistic approach.

With humanism, we are edging closer to the elusive goal of fully understanding how to develop creativity in learners. And yet, we are still not quite there. The teacher relating to learners in accordance with humanistic principles is creating the *preconditions* for developing creative learners, but they will not be enough by themselves to actually bring it about.

To nurture creativity, the teacher needs to somehow get learner to make coherent sense of problems presented to them. This involves facilitating a process which involves taking *fragments* – objects, facts, thoughts, images etc. that mean nothing on their own – and connecting them so as to form meaningful patterns and coherent wholes. Another way of saying this is that we are trying to get them to assemble clues in such a way that they tell a story, much like a detective trying to solve a crime.

The first psychologists to study this process systematically were members of the gestalt school: Wolfgang Kohler (1929), Max Wertheimer (1910-1943, 1959), and Kurt Koffka (1935). These theorists set themselves up in opposition to behaviourism, the dominant paradigm in psychology at the time. Their central critique of behaviourism was that it assumed that we could understand even the most complex human behaviour patterns by breaking them down into discreet elements and identifying the stimulus-response relationship responsible for each element. Once we have done this, according to behaviourism, we can teach any human being to perform any skill at all by conditioning her to perform each element separately and then piecing the elements together; the whole is simply the sum of its parts.

The gestaltists, on the other hand, asserted that the whole is always *greater than* the sum of any of its parts because the whole contains meaning. For real learning to take place, the learner needs to do much more than master the individual elements of a skill or a field of understanding; she needs in addition to grasp how these individual elements come together in a way that *makes sense*. Kohler in particular uses the term 'insight learning' to refer to the way in which learners reorganise the elements before them in new ways so as to create new insights which form the bases of genuine understanding. Here, then, is the essence of the creativity we have been searching for.

In terms of educational practice, gestalt pushes teachers towards giving learners the autonomy and freedom they need to put things together in their own way. It is not for the teacher to say, *"You do this, then you do that, and then you'll have the correct answer."*, or, *"No, not like that – that's wrong!"* Rather, the teacher provides experiences and supplies information, and then allows the learner to decide how these things should be combined to create understandings. Such an approach requires enormous faith in the learner's ability to think for himself and in his motivation to succeed, as well as in his resourcefulness at coming up with different ideas until he finds the one that works. The teacher also needs to have the patience to give it the time it needs.

One subject where a gestalt approach does, I think, work wonderfully well is mathematics. I would say that real mathematics is predominantly about holistic thinking, pattern-spotting and meaning-making, as would be implied by gestalt theory. Yet it is all too often taught as if it were an assortment of unconnected mechanical drills and reduced to soulless number crunching. Learners on the receiving end of such an uninspiring approach start to think of maths as boring and difficult, and too many of them become alienated from the subject. I was one such when I was at school. But it is not difficult to teach maths lessons that are about being creative; you just supply the raw materials from which learners can build things and the clues they can use to solve problems.

I did not enjoy school. Not for me back then the buzz of excitement of trying to solve a problem or the shiver of euphoria when the sudden insight hit me. I played the game and jumped through the hoops because my family expected me to, and because I knew it was in my best interests to do so. I was never particularly creative, except perhaps in English compositions, and I relied heavily on set routines given to me by teachers as well as on my ability to memorize chunks of information I didn't really understand. I did okay at school, but I did not find academia truly inspiring until many years after my formal education ended. That was when it dawned on me that everything in the world was connected to everything else and that academic study was a way of understanding those connections and what they meant. After that, knowledge and understanding became a thrilling adventure for me and has never stopped being so.

Creativity involves a sort of freeing up of the mind, a cultivation of cognitive *flexibility*. I have always been intrigued by the connection between creativity and humour. Humour clearly has a role to play in creating a relaxed atmosphere which makes learners feel safe enough to take risks, but is there more to it than this? It seems to me that what connects humour to creativity is *inversion* – turning normal assumptions inside out, upside down and back to front.

The French philosopher Henri Bergson argued (1911) that laughter arises from behaviour that is seen by others as inflexible, mechanistic and routinised. This has some resonance for me as a driving instructor; the behaviour of learner drivers is often hilarious for this very reason. At its simplest level, learning is about developing habits and routines which are initially performed in a clumsy, jerky sort of way, as if the learner were a robot. But learning needs to progress beyond this. The learner needs to become more flexible, more nuanced, in a word, more *human* in how they apply their newly-learnt skills. Bergson's theory implies that humour is critical in making this transition, that the learner needs to be able to let go and laugh, particularly at himself. This in turn allows him to relax and hand over control to his brain's automatic pilot – its *default mode network*. The truth of this is certainly borne out in my experience; I tend to find that it is those learners who get angry and frustrated with their lack of fluidity, rather than having a sense of humour over it, who struggle most to make progress.

The importance of humour in learning perhaps becomes clearer when we consider how the human brain responds to new challenges. We owe much of our understanding in this area to the work of Donald Hebb (1949). The brain is made up of some 86 billion individual neurones capable of interconnecting in all sorts of different patterns or 'neural networks'. Any given human activity requiring brain power, be it playing chess, solving an equation or cooking an omelette, will require the activation of the necessary neural networks. Once formed, neural networks strengthen with use and become easier to slip into. This equates to the use of what I have previously referred to as mental maps. But what happens when the brain is presented with a completely new challenge for which the pre-existing neural networks are inadequate? Clearly, new networks need to be created, but is there any way of nurturing this process - priming the brain – so that any given individual might become better at it?

The psychologist Edward de Bono (1970), in a train of reasoning that I think dovetails well both with Hebb's work and Bergson's theory, argues that the first step in getting the mind to generate a new thought pattern is to say something that does not make sense, i.e. to make a joke. New understanding emerges as a bi-product of getting the joke. Consider this one:

'Did you hear about the statistician who drowned crossing the river?

He knew that it was three feet deep, on average.'

Taken from https://www.fatherly.com/play/math-jokes-and-math-puns/ Accessed 02/07/2020.

The new understanding to emerge, of course, is that averages tell us nothing about the individual measurements from which they are compiled. This is an example of *insight learning*, and is exactly what we should be aspiring to achieve in education – the development of the ability in learners to create entirely new understandings rather than having to search their memory banks to find old ones which might just about do. If learners are in an environment where jokes and humour are commonplace, their brains are being primed to readily adopt new ways of thinking in response to new challenges, and I genuinely believe that the art of comedy should be part of the curriculum for any reputable teacher training course.

De Bono insists that the ability to think creatively has nothing to do with a person's level of inherited intelligence, or IQ. In fact, when we use the term 'IQ', what we are referring to is an individual's ability to perform *convergent thinking* – using logic to answer the sorts of questions that have only one answer. This is indeed a largely inherited ability that some people are naturally better at than others. However, creativity is much more reliant on *divergent thinking* – coming up with lots of possible answers to the sorts of questions that don't have one specific answer. This distinction is a crucial issue in the world of formal education where the prevailing (and very damaging) assumption is that, if a person's IQ falls below a certain level, we cannot expect too much of them beyond following simple instructions. On the contrary, De Bono maintains, creative thinking is a skill that can be mastered just like any other – by paying attention to it and practising. On the basis of my experience, I fully support this. In fact, I would go as far as to argue that, if a learner has a lower than average IQ, all the more reason to give him the opportunity to learn to think creatively.

De Bono bemoans the fact that most people make the mistake of trying to think too quickly. As a result, they tend to jump to obvious conclusions rather than exploring lots of alternatives and choosing the best one. There are a great many success stories to be found of people finding alternative solutions to problems that turn out to be better than the obvious one. Think, for example, of James Dyson's cyclonic vacuum cleaner or Alec Issigonis's transverse engine. Teachers need to encourage learners to think in terms of exploring alternatives and to give them the time to do this. One of the most enjoyable things about mathematics is the leisurely contemplation of a problem in which different strategies are tried out in thought experiments. Often, it is when one lets go of a particular way of thinking and adopts a new one that one experiences that *eureka!* moment. This, after all, is how real mathematicians work.

De Bono's term for being able to switch between different ways of thinking in response to unfamiliar situations is 'lateral thinking', and he suggests that one way of making ourselves think laterally is to deliberately contemplate ideas that seem at first glance to be absurd or irrational. As one thinks through the idea, one begins to realise that it is perhaps not as absurd as one had assumed. This was how Einstein came up with his theories of relativity, and I would imagine that the person who first proposed democracy as a viable system of government was considered insane by his contemporaries. I would add that such 'off the wall' ideas are often gifts from the unconscious minds that are then developed consciously. Sir Paul McCartney, for example, is on record as saying that the melody of his song *Yesterday* came to him in a dream. If we want to develop in learners the ability to approach problems creatively and flexibly, as opposed to following set routines, we need to allow them to play and to

43

daydream, to free them occasionally from structure and goal-directed activity.

Learners also need the space to *experiment* – to try, to fail, to keep trying until they succeed. I am not necessarily saying that teachers shouldn't tell learners things – facts, theories and so on – but there is a big difference between this and instructing them on how to use the information to solve the problem. Wherever possible, and within reason, *get them to do it for themselves.*

To return once again to the emotional aspect of being human, to be creative, a person needs to *feel like* being creative. As a student once said to me when I had criticised her English composition for its lack of creativity, *"It's hard to be creative when you're hungry."* Things like hunger, pain and tiredness kill the desire to be creative and, as we have seen, so do fear and anxiety. However, there is another way of looking at the relationship between anxiety/fear and creativity. The psychoanalyst Donald Winnicott (1953) argued that the function of play was to allow the individual to explore the boundaries between consciousnesses and the dark, hidden world of the unconscious and, to be willing to do this, she needs to feel safe enough. If the individual is a child, it is the responsibility of the adult caregiver to try to create such an emotionally safe environment, but if the environment is *too* safe, if the child is over-protected and doesn't get a chance to explore the dark side of her own mind, this is counter-productive to healthy emotional development. Winnicott used the term 'good enough mother' to describe the caregiver who gets the balance more or less right between providing too much and too little anxiety but, in dealing with learners in formal education, we could perhaps talk of 'good enough teachers', teachers who sensitively push learners towards their fears.

At this point, it might be worthwhile drawing a distinction between *playfulness* and *creativity.* Creativity is playfulness allied to an acceptance of reality and a sense of responsibility. Playfulness, by contrast, is a feature of infancy which can be thought of as a sort of training in creativity, one in which the child learns to come to terms with whatever makes him anxious or fearful. As a result, he gradually learns to be comfortable with reality and doesn't constantly run away from it. In this way, his playfulness evolves into genuine creativity. I believe that, if children experience the right sort of relationship with their teacher at an early age, one that gets the balance between push and protect more or less right most of the time, they will become increasingly capable of dealing with both the reality within their own minds and the reality of the world around them, so that by the time they reach adolescence and early adulthood, being creative in the true sense will be the most natural thing in the world for them. If, on the other hand, a child is not fortunate enough to have this sort of relationship with at least one other person as he's growing up, he might well try to compensate in adolescence or adulthood by being playful *as opposed* to creative, striving always to escape reality and avoid responsibility through fantasy or infantile behaviour.

We live in a world where we are confronted by a great existential threat – the destruction of the natural environment. This is our reality, the thing for which we must take responsibility, the thing to which we must apply our creativity. Sadly, we are hampered in this by our steadfast refusal to let go of deeply ingrained, centuries old ways of thinking: 'the natural world is there to be exploited', 'economic growth is always a good thing', 'if something doesn't have economic value then it is worthless', and so on. We desperately need new ideas; we need to be able to look at our world afresh, to reconceptualise what it is, reformulate what it means to us, reimagine how we relate to it. The need for creativity is urgent and becoming increasingly desperate.

Chapter 3

Narrative and Learning

We have seen that people learn by creatively putting fragments together to make wholes and also that, to become creative, they need to be given opportunities to use imagination to explore their deepest fears and anxieties. One of the oldest and most widespread ways of combining these two factors is *story-telling*. When I was at primary school, this would be done by getting the pupils to sit in a semi-circle and telling them a story, but it can just as easily done by showing them a movie. Showing the right film or telling the right story to the right group at the right time can facilitate sudden jumps in understanding, especially if the teacher is skilled at encouraging the learners to engage with the narrative by interpreting and explaining the events described.

There is nothing wrong with allowing learners to occasionally sit back and be an audience. On the other hand, learners may feel safe enough, with a bit of sensitive pushing, to get involved in actually devising and/or performing their own narratives. One way of doing this is through role-play, whether scripted, semi-scripted or fully improvised, in which learners act out scenarios developed from situations they are familiar with.

There is clearly a close interrelationship between the mind's ability to construct narratives, its ability to form episodic memories, and its ability to imagine possible futures. Episodic memory should not be thought of as a set of accurate records of experiences but as *interpretations* of experiences – attempts to give them meaning. By interpreting her past in a negative way: *"I always fail"*, *"I'm always the victim"*, *"I'm so stupid"*, and so on, an individual restricts the possible futures she imagines for herself: *"I will always fail"*, *"I will always be a victim"*, *"I will always be stupid"*. A skilled teacher would address this issue by encouraging the learner to re-interpret the stories she tells about herself in such a way that she creates a more positive self-image. This could be done through the written word, but also through painting/drawing, drama or music. This is precisely what is being attempted in the NLP technique of re-framing, described earlier.

Helping learners to re-construct their self-concept so that they have an expanded view of what they are capable of is what great teachers do. The novel *A Kestrel for a Knave* by Barry Hines (1969) tells the story of Billy Casper, a working class teen with a difficult home life who finds a sense of escape through rearing and training a young hawk. Learning to do this demands considerable time, effort and intellectual capacity on the part of Billy, and yet at his school he is considered a low-achiever, a problem pupil even. In one scene, he turns up for his English class late, having just been caned by the headmaster for sleeping in assembly. His initial demeanour his negative and defensive, but the teacher, Mr. Farthing, shows great sensitivity and skill in getting him to open up and talk about himself, doing this by showing an interest in Billy's falconry hobby and getting him to explain aspects of it to the class. Teaching like this might seem easy to an onlooker, but is in reality anything but. It is not something that can be taught in any conventional sense, nor is it a natural gift that you either have or you don't. This level of mastery comes from intense reflection on experience and relentless self-questioning.

People who are good at memorising long lists of unrelated items understand that the secret to this is not repetition, as many assume, but *association*. What these memory athletes do is connect the items on their lists in such a way as to make them tell stories. It seems as if the human brain is somehow hard-wired to understand concepts as dramatic scenarios in which protagonists pit their wits against obstacles in pursuit of their goals. We have known this for a very long time. In Ancient Athens, for example, it was seen as part of a citizen's civic duty to attend the theatre so as to be educated in the great philosophical themes dealt with in the plays they saw. The citizens of Athens undoubtedly remembered what they had learnt in a much deeper and long-lasting sense than would have been the case if they had been made to sit through lectures. The memory associated with the story is especially likely to stick when the we feel *emotion* in connection with the scenario, when we *care* about the success or otherwise of the protagonist.

There are times when might substitute the word 'context' for 'story'. When we speak of understanding an event *in context*, what we mean is understanding the part the event plays in the story of which it is an integral part, as opposed to understanding it purely as a thing in itself. In teaching mathematics, for example, we *could* present subjects such as fractions, algebra, trigonometry etc. as discreet entities to be understood on their own terms. But an alternative way would be to invent a story in which a particular individual needed to solve a number of problems in order to achieve a goal, each of the problems requiring the application of a particular field of mathematical understanding. In the former approach, the learner may fail to commit the pieces of learning to memory because she has no narrative to tag them to or context in which to place them. However, in the latter approach there is a good chance that the learner will remember the story, especially if it is dramatic and has some resonance to her own life.

While people of all ages enjoy stories, different types of story and ways of telling them are appropriate to different stages in the learner's development. Writing from a psychoanalytic perspective, Bettelheim (1976) argues that fairy tales are important in the *emotional* development of young children because they are externalisations of intensely emotional dramas being played out in the unconscious realms of the mind, dramas to do with personal desires coming up against the need for acceptance and approval. Engagement with such stories is part of the process through which a person ultimately becomes rational – capable of controlling his emotions and handling reality. According to Bettelheim, it is quite wrong for adults to interfere with the process by imposing their own meanings of the stories onto children, or to try to protect them from distress by sanitising them. It is also, he believes, better to *tell* the child the story and let her use her imagination to generate images to go with it than to rob her of this opportunity through illustration or animation.

Using stories in this way allows teachers to approach universal psychological themes – suspicion of the other, fear of the unknown, masculinity and femininity, unequal power relations – early in the child's emotional development and raises the possibility that the manifestations of these themes which tend to emerge later – racism, sexism and so on – might be prevented by early intervention.

Whilst we may initially encounter stories as told through words, our brains seem to have a way of turning them into visual images so as to create, to borrow a phrase used in radio broadcasting, a *theatre of the mind*. Using the imagination to convert words to images is easy, especially if one gets lots of opportunity to practise, but doing the reverse is much harder. So much effort in education seems to go into trying to get learners to put ideas and feelings into words, to explain everything so that it makes logical sense. It is as if there is an assumption that the logico-linguistic way of thinking is the only legitimate mode there is.

When I first started teaching, I was fascinated by the role of the spoken word in learning because I saw learning as essentially the internalisation of a spoken dialogue. But this, I have since come to realise, is a very limited way of understanding the learning process. I have no doubt that words and sentences are a useful way of structuring and systematising thoughts, and for conveying logical precision. However, through my interest in cinema and theatre, I have come to appreciate that there is a language of visual imagery which has the power to speak to the unconscious mind in a way that words cannot.

Expressing knowledge in words, then, should not be thought of as the be-all-and-end-all of education, and we should be wary of becoming obsessed with getting learners to constantly do this. If they become conditioned to expect to have to verbalise their responses to experiences at some future point in time, they will be thinking about this chore whilst they are meant to be having the experience instead of just having the experience. University students will be familiar with this phenomenon; during a lecture they scribble away on their note pads, desperately trying to record each and every point the lecturer makes, and then the lecture ends with them not having understood a word of it. They would get much more out of the lecture if they left their pens and notebooks in their bags and just gave themselves over to the experience.

Instead of always demanding verbal or written responses to things, we sometimes need to just expose learners to an experience, let them respond spontaneously to that, and then just leave it there. Consider the following scenario:

Teacher: (to a class of primary school children). Next Thursday we're going on a trip.

Class: Hurrah!

Teacher: We're going to London.

Class: Hurrah!

Teacher: We'll be going on the London Eye. Then we'll go to the Tower of London and Madame Tussaud's.

Class: Hurrah!

Teacher: And you'll need to take notes because you'll be writing a report about the trip when you return to school the next day.

Class: (Silence).

The children won't enjoy the trip as much as they should because they will spend the whole day making notes *about* experiences they are theoretically having rather than properly *having* the experiences. Educationally, it would have been a missed opportunity. If the teacher wants the pupils to discuss the experiences retrospectively, why doesn't she just take photos and use those, or just rely on the pupils' memories?

Here's another example. A learner driver is progressing towards test readiness, so the instructor decides to carry out a mock test. Instead of just driving, as they had been doing up to this point, and doing it very well, the learner starts to have a conversation with herself about whether they are driving correctly, and doing it in a slightly time-delayed way, so they are constantly thinking about what happened a few seconds ago and putting the experiences into words. As a result, they lose the ability to think and act spontaneously in the present moment and make mistake after mistake. Instead of just *doing*, they are *thinking about what they're doing.*

53

Too much emphasis on logico-linguistic thinking turns a lot of children off formal education. It makes them uptight and anxious, worried about having to explain why they do things, fearful of the consequences of not being able to do it. They learn to memorise sequences and trot out pre-rehearsed explanations rather than how to think for themselves. The ones who are not good at this will start to compare themselves unfavourably with the ones who are and to hate themselves for not being as good as them. Fun and learning turn into fear and loathing. Children such afflicted will start to find meaningful, 'in the moment' experiences outside of school, through music perhaps, or in experimenting with drugs. Pete Townshend of *The Who* summed this up in the lyrics of the song *I Can't Explain* – the attitude of being too busy experiencing life in the raw to be able to summon up the energy and focus to explain and analyse.

We should not, then, be overkeen to privilege the logico-linguistic over the visual. The word 'visual' in the sense that I am using it here, should not be taken too literally, however. What I am warning against is the tendency to use language to analyse experience a moment after it takes place, thus missing the essence of the experience itself, but language can be used to create or express in-the-moment experiences; songs, poems and jokes are three good examples. Touchy/feely hands-on experiences also count as 'visual' in this context. The word simply denotes an emphasis on immediate experience and spontaneous gut reactions.

In the west, there is a deeply ingrained belief that all human activity must be directed towards an explicit goal or purpose, that it cannot be of value in itself. However, an experience does not need to be purposeful to be meaningful. In mathematics, for example, we make the distinction between applied maths, where the meaning is bound up with purpose and pure maths where meaning exists devoid of practical applicability. This does not make pure mathematics a waste of time. If an experience is meaningful, i.e. the experiencer is able to find personal meaning in it, then it is educational and requires no for purpose, no explanatory 'why'. Creative people in fields such as painting, music, theatre and cinema have no problem grasping this. They are wary about explaining their work, even to themselves, and don't expect the public to be able to explain it in order to appreciate it; it is what it is. Teachers need to grasp this idea too and apply it in their own work. It is undoubtedly true that learners learn *from* experience, that is by reflecting on and analysing experiences. But they also learn *in* experience where their unconscious minds are doing the analysis for them and they don't need to make any conscious effort to learn.

Of course, we cannot discard logical analysis altogether. Let's imagine a group of primitive cave-dwellers trying to hunt down a wild animal for food. We can imagine the group being split along the lines of those who advocate taking time out to discuss the situation and devise a strategy and those who argue that this would just waste time and what they really should be doing is getting after the animal before it's had a chance to get too far away. Both points of view have equal validity and the group's leader would need to find a way of achieving the best of both worlds. When I'm teaching, I'm in a similar position. On the one hand, I'm encouraging the learner to think about and understand the situation they're faced with before leaping to action (logico-linguistic analysis), but on the other I'm discouraging them from getting so bogged down in analysis that they are inhibited from just 'having a go'. This is true whether I'm teaching someone maths, how to drive a car or anything else.

Logico-linguistic analysis is incredibly useful, either before or after an experience, but it can never be a substitute for experience, and it needs to be no more complicated than it needs to be. When we do use it, we need a way of combining as much visual imagery as possible with only as much analysis as necessary. One method of achieving this is through Tony Buzan's (1993) 'Mind Maps' approach. Here, the learner creates a visual map of the subject or skill she is learning. This could be thought of as a physical, externalised form of the sort of mental map discussed in the last chapter. The mind map is composed of discrete elements, but it simultaneously joins the elements together with lines or arrows to show the connections between the elements and so form a coherent system of understanding – a story if you like. This idea, of bringing together discreet elements to form wholes, is strongly reminiscent of gestalt. The beauty of the method is that it allows for systematisation whilst at the same time employing the immediacy and impact potential of the visual, thus achieving the best of both worlds.

A very different take on the role of story-telling in education comes to light when we start to think about education in political terms. From this perspective, the central question is whether the learner allows himself to be the subject of narratives created for him by others or gets the opportunity to become the author of his own narratives. This is where the idea of *voice*, of a person speaking her own truth and having it listened to – comes in. If an individual can develop, or be helped to develop, her own unique voice, whether through the spoken word, the written word, art, music, sport, through whatever medium he/she feels drawn to, she moves towards becoming the author of her own narrative, and thus of her own identity. She becomes not an objective 'thing' to be manipulated but a thinking subject with free will.

Every time a teacher says to a learner, or group of learners, *"Shut up and listen to me."*, he is sending them the message that the only voice that matters is his. If, however, he gives learners a chance to speak and voice their opinions, he is affirming their right to be free-thinking individuals. Of course, this can only work if each learner affords the same respect to his fellow learners and to the teacher. It is an ideal state of affairs to be worked towards by means of developing an atmosphere based on acceptance, genuineness and empathy.

Chapter 4

Individual Learning Style

The more I understand about the brain and the nervous system, the more I see learning as a struggle to get the performance of a new skill away from the regions of the brain involved in conscious effort towards the automatic pilot regions. The quicker a learner can do this, the more the conscious part of the brain is freed up for paying attention to new learning. This transition is achieved through practice (the experiential aspect) and reflection (the analytical aspect). Learning requires both, but my experience is that individual learners differ in the optimal balance between the two. I, for example, like short bursts of practice interspersed with long periods of reflection when I'm learning something new, while for others that ratio is reversed. Everyone is somewhere or other on that spectrum, and this brings us to the topic of individual learning style.

If we take it as a given that every learner has a unique personal identity, it is a logical step from here to taking seriously the notion that each individual has a preferred learning style. If we go along with this, part of the teacher's job must be to identify the individual learning style of each learner and use this knowledge in lesson planning. A great many theorists have written about learning style, often pushing their own personal theories about it; if any given learner could be said to have a preferred learning style, any given teacher could be said to have a preferred *theory* about preferred learning styles. The simplest of these explain it in binary terms: concrete v abstract, left-brained v right-brained and so on. However, one of the most widely used theories is known as the VAK model and was developed by the same Bandler & Grinder partnership that came up with NLP. It uses a typology of what the authors claim to be three discernible styles: *visual*, *auditory* and *kinaesthetic* (hence VAK). If we accept their premise that the brain is like a computer, we can think of the visual, auditory and kinaesthetic modes of perception as its three principle data input portals. It just so happens, according to the theory, that any given learner tends to have a strong preference for one of the three.

Gardner (1983) ups the ante by proposing the existence of 'multiple intelligences' (eight in total): visuo-spatial, linguistic-verbal, logical-mathematical, bodily-kinaesthetic, musical, interpersonal, intrapersonal, and naturalistic. A typical individual would have a unique profile of strengths and weaknesses and, armed with each learner's profile as revealed by an initial assessment, the teacher should prepare activities for each learner which reflect that learner's strengths. In contrast with the concept of IQ, which suggests a natural hierarchy based on a genetic inheritance of *one kind of* intelligence, Gardner's model is more egalitarian; if there are multiple inherited intelligences, who is to judge issues of natural superiority/inferiority? It is a very attractive model for precisely that reason.

We can also make inferences about how individual learners might prefer to be treated based on their personality types. Eysenck (1990), for example, argues that individuals can be assigned personality profiles based on their positions on two axes: introversion/extroversion and neuroticism. Eysenck did not develop his model to be used specifically in educational contexts, but an individual's personality profile could be expected to have a significant bearing on the kind of learning environment she does best in. A good teacher would naturally take this into account in lesson planning and would endeavour to cater, for example, both for introverts requiring time for quiet reflection and extroverts requiring social interaction. She would also be careful not to push a highly neurotic individual too far out of his comfort zone.

But are we in danger, perhaps, of taking the concept of individual learning style too far? I would argue that placing too much emphasis on *individual* learning style puts us in danger of losing sight of the essentially *social* nature of so much learning, the ways in which learners learn together and learn from each other. Thinking in terms of individual learning style might be very apt when we are considering the individual learner working alone while engaged in a particular learning activity, but when we are considering a learning process involving multiple individuals it is perhaps better to think more in terms of a group learning style. A good analogy here is a football team; yes, the individual team members have their own unique qualities and should express themselves as individuals, but not at the expense of undermining the playing style of the team as a whole. I think that, if there is enough empathy in the classroom, learners will tend to adapt their own learning style to accommodate other learners in the group.

We can also think of in terms of teachers and learners meeting each other halfway. A teacher and a learner come together and form a relationship. Each brings something to that relationship; the learner brings a preferred learning style and the teacher a preferred teaching style. As in any successful relationship, each partner unconsciously adapts to the other. I reject the idea that the teacher has a duty to slavishly serve the learner's learning style regardless of her own preferred teaching style. This reduces the teacher-learner relationship to an economic transaction in which the learner is the customer and the teacher the supplier of a service.

At time of writing, I have been thus far unable to uncover anything in the way of convincing empirical evidence to suggest that individuals are biologically pre-programmed with particular *learning styles*, along the lines of, say, the VAK model. I think it is much more likely that individuals develop the learning styles that go with the particular thing they have needed to learn at any given time. If we accept this argument, then it should be perfectly possible for learners to adopt new learning styles when they need to learn different things, and it is perfectly reasonable for teachers to expect and encourage them to do so. For a learner to say, *"I expect you to teach me in a way that is compatible with my pre-existing*

61

learning style" is tantamount to saying, *"I want to learn but I don't want to go out of my comfort zone"*. It just doesn't work like that. Clearly, by refusing to gently pushing learners beyond their comfort zones in terms of preferred learning style, we are denying them opportunities for intellectual growth.

Differentiating learners from one another and allowing them to each learn in their own way makes a lot of sense where there is a cultural tradition of uniformity and social compliance which needs to be counter-balanced. It definitely makes sense in situations where learners have difficulties in learning that are unique to them as individuals, whether physical, psychological, neurological or socio-economic, and need to be given a level playing field. However, we need to remember that, in non-compulsory education, learners have already differentiated themselves by choosing to enrol on their course and are often explicitly looking for a social experience and/or be taken out of their comfort zone. Personally, if I decided to become a student, I'd be surprised and disappointed if the teacher said to me, *"I've assessed you as being an auditory learner so you're going to sit with the other auditory learners doing auditory activities"*. If that did happen, I'd feel cheated out of the chance to interact with people who were different from me and of the chance to explore new ways of learning.

We also need to consider the sheer impracticability of being obsessed with learners' individual idiosyncrasies; teachers are human beings and there is only so much they can realistically be expected to do in terms of preparation. A burnt-out teacher is of no use to any learner. I think that a sensible approach is to acknowledging individual difference is to prepare for the whole group with the expectation that everyone will participate in everything, but to make sure that there are things built into the lesson which appeal to as many different learning styles/preferences as possible.

More important than differentiation in terms of teaching methodologies and modes of presenting information is differentiation in terms of how we relate to learners – having the sensitivity to realise that different individuals respond to different communication styles. For example, should you be an encouraging friend or a harsh critic? What sort of sense of humour do they have? Do they like it when you share personal information with them, or do they want you to stick to the matter in hand? You often find these things out by keeping your mouth shut, taking a back seat, listening and observing, and then reflecting back on what you hear and see. Doing this, I believe, develops what Goleman (1995) calls 'emotional intelligence' (EI) and this, I think, is a different concept from that of mental health. Having good mental health, it seems to me, is the absence of something bad, i.e. a psychological disorder, whereas EI is the presence of something good, i.e. a highly attuned capacity for empathy with others. With people who have very high EI it is as if they have so much psychological health that they can afford to donate some to others. Unlike personality type, which is relatively fixed for any given individual, EI can be consciously worked on and increased. Of course, the biggest advantage of relating to learners in an emotionally intelligent way is that they themselves are unconsciously developing their own emotional intelligence through the process.

For me, *intelligence* is the ability to draw together different capacities for the purposes of problem-solving. It is therefore by definition general rather than specific; someone who is 'intelligent' has a whole range of different capacities. If a learner has become over-reliant on a narrow range of thinking or learning styles, then perhaps the best thing a teacher can do for that learner is to encourage him to extend his range. The fact that people tend to become comfortable with using their brain in one particular way does not mean that they are incapable of learning others.

Much as I may come across as being sceptical where it comes to individual learning style, I have no objection teachers to using one of the numerous individual learning style models *if it works for them*. Teachers ought to regard themselves as practitioner-researchers, testing out theories and ideas in the laboratory of their own classroom. Moreover, sometimes things just work because we *believe* that they will work. This is because, if we believe that something will work, we will apply it with much more intensity and conviction than a sceptic would, and we will be more prone to interpret the outcomes in a positive light, attributing any perceived successes to the method. If a teacher finds that a particular approach works for them, does it really matter if there is no rigorous empirical evidence to support it? Well, If a teacher wants to quietly use it in her own practice, then no, it doesn't matter. But if she wants to go on the evangelical trail and persuade other teachers to drop what works for them and adopt her approach, then it does matter, especially if the one doing the evangelising occupies a position of power relative to those she is trying to impose her ideas on.

What is really needed is a professional culture within schools and colleges in which it is the norm for teachers to read and discuss the research evidence for themselves, form tentative hypotheses about what methods are likely to work, and then test them in their own classrooms. This kind of cultural shift requires as a prerequisite an influx of a particular type of person into teaching. I would describe such a person as contemplative, questioning and, in the most positive sense of the word, *introverted* (see Cain, 2012). It also needs those teachers already in the profession who are inclined to that way of thinking to find their voices more, hopefully supported in that by their more extraverted colleagues.

The idea that learners, if encouraged, can develop new learning styles brings us to the phenomenon known as neuroplasticity. I viewed with fascination a TED talk given by Dr. Lara Boyd (14/11/2015), a researcher on the rehabilitation of stroke victims, on the subject. Neuroplasticity is the tendency of the brain to change chemically, structurally and functionally in response to new challenges. I think that neuroplasticity helps to explain 'plateauing' in the learning process; the pauses in the learner's progress make sense if we realise that the initial rapid progress is due to chemical changes in the brain which can take place very quickly but that, in order maintain progress, to move to higher levels of competence, structural changes need to take place, and these changes take time. If we see the brain as analogous to a house, short-term rapid learning is like using more of its existing rooms to accommodate a growing number of occupants, but there comes a point where the house is crammed full and the only way to fit more people in is to build an extension.

Dr Boyd's research seems to indicate that, while practice matters enormously in the learning of a new skill, different individuals' brains will change in different ways. I think that this partially explains the existence of different learning styles and why learners vary greatly in how fast they learn, but it also implies that the brain of any given individual is wonderfully adaptable in terms of learning and will usually get there in the end.

It makes intuitive sense to me to try to make classroom practice reflect the way the brain works. One aspect of brain specialisation that particularly fascinates me is the difference in function between the left and right cerebral hemispheres. In the 1960s, Michael Gazzaniga, in collaboration with Roger Sperry and Joseph Bogen, conducted a series of experiments on human split-brain subjects – individuals who had had their corpus callosums, the bodies connecting the two halves of their brains, severed in an operation to control their epilepsy (Gazzaniga, 1970 and 2005). The researchers realised that, if a way could be found of delivering information to one side of the brain of a split-brain subject but not the other, this would allow them to study the implications of having a split-brain and that this in turn would lead to new insights into the functioning of a normal brain.

By using a screen capable of flashing up words and images either on the left or on the right, the researchers set up a situation in which visual information could be delivered to the subject's brain either exclusively through their left eye (i.e. to their right brain) or through their right eye (i.e. to their left brain). The subject sat at a desk facing the screen and focussed on a dot at its centre. When information flashed up on the right of the screen, it was picked up by the subject's right eye and entered the left side of their brain. When it flashed up on the left, it entered the right side of the brain. In one version of the experiment, information in the form of a word was delivered to the subject's left brain. It was found that the subject could say the word without difficulty. However, when a word was delivered to the subject's right brain, they could not say the word, but could draw a picture of the thing that the word signified. Once the image was on the paper in front of them, they could see it with both eyes and, because their left brain had now been let in on the secret, they were able to say the word.

Through this and other similar experiments, it became apparent that the two halves of a split-brain have different characteristics. You might almost describe them as two different people, each with his/her own personality. What emerges is a picture of the brain that is fundamentally asymmetrical. In particular, the left brain is the language and logic centre whilst the right is better at visuo-spatial processing and thinking holistically. A teacher needs to be able to appeal to both sides of the learner's brain, but also to encourage learners to develop and use both sides in a collaborative fashion.

Of all the individual learning style theories, the one I find most useful is the one that characterises people as either predominantly left-brained or right-brained. This is because a two-part classification system is cleaner and simpler, and therefore easier to use, than one which uses three or more categories. A left-brained approach to learning a new skill would be to break it down into its constituent sub-skills and to express what each sub-skill involves in precise, linguistic terms. A right-brained strategy would be to visualise the skill as a complete whole and imagine oneself performing the skill. I don't know if people are *genetically* biased towards one or the other, but I believe they can develop a bias through life experience.

It is easy for a teacher to fall into the trap of trying to force the strategy that worked for them when they were learning the skill onto the learner they are trying to teach and then get frustrated when the learner doesn't respond well to this. Why not switch to a right-brained approach when a left-brained one Isn't working or a left-brained approach in the opposite scenario?

There are times when using pictures and encouraging learners to be creative works very well, but there are other times when what is required in clear verbal explanation. These switches can be made quite spontaneously in the midst of a lesson.

At other times, the problem is that the learner himself persists doggedly with a strategy that no longer works, leading to a learning impasse where a learner who has made rapid progress in the initial stages of learning suddenly stalls because of a reluctance to switch strategies, either from right to left-brained or vice versa. The way forward from this is for the learner to tell himself a different story about who he is, about how he approaches problems and about what he's capable of.

Chapter 5

To Learn or Not to Learn

This chapter is largely concerned with the unconscious mind. For the knowledge I have in this area, I owe much to the work of the psychiatrist and hypnotherapist Milton H. Erickson (1901-1980), in particular his book *Healing in Hypnosis* (1983).

Most people would say that, from time to time, they just *know* something without knowing why they know it. This feeling *can* come from genuine intuition, that is from an independent source of wisdom in the psyche of the individual. But it can also come from subliminal manipulation of the type used by advertisers or those with a political message to push, or else from the residues of hurtful past experiences which create sudden intense emotions.

As a driving instructor, I have sat in the back seat for numerous driving tests. It never fails to amaze me how many candidates drive perfectly well until the last few minutes of the test and then cause themselves to fail by committing a silly error. It is as if the unconscious mind of the individual, for reasons of its own, does not want them to pass at that particular time, perhaps does not believe they deserve to pass at that particular time, and so sabotages the test. But it can work the other way as well, where I am virtually sure that the person will fail, but something inside them takes control and gets them through to a successful outcome.

The unconscious can exert its influence in all sorts of positive ways. For example, in the course of my teaching career, I have frequently experienced a phenomenon in which a learner makes a sudden leap, as opposed to a gradual improvement, in their ability. One possible explanation for this is that their unconscious mind is working on the issues all the time, even when conscious attention is focused elsewhere. When the unconscious mind reaches a conclusion, it throws this conclusion into consciousness in the form of a sudden breakthrough in understanding.

This process, what we might call unconscious *incubation*, can take years. In one of her televised performances (streamed on UK Netflix, 2020), the comedian Sarah Silverman told an anecdote about how, when she was a child, she had taken acting lessons. The teacher had said to her, *"Acting is re-acting"*. She did not understand what this meant at the time but, many years later, as an adult, she was in her car at a red light waiting for it to change. Then she suddenly understood what her acting teacher had meant: *acting is reacting*. When it comes to learning, I think that our unconscious minds generally know things well in advance of our conscious minds and throw them into consciousness when we are ready for them, not before.

In Chapter 1, I said that learning and the motivation to learn go hand-in-hand. This is true enough, but we need to be aware that the true motivation for any given choice of action may be unconscious, and that a distinction can be made between what the unconscious mind instructs the body to do and what the conscious mind fabricates to explain away the action *post hoc.* For example, someone might explain to himself his hostility towards another person in terms of that other person's pernicious character, when the real reason is unconscious envy.

The unconscious can be thought of as a sort of hidden self, an alter-ego. It can be helpful and protective, but it can also throw up barriers to learning in the form of 'ego defence mechanisms' (Anna Freud, 1937) –

psychological strategies through which the unconscious protects the conscious mind from anxiety. Here are a few of them:

In *displacement*, an individual re-directs feelings such as anger away from its original source, for example a parent, onto a safer alternative, for example a teacher. Much of the unprovoked aggression towards teachers can, I believe, be explained in this way, particularly where the learner has unhealthy relationships elsewhere in his life.

In *projection*, an individual takes a particular quality about himself that causes him guilt or shame and projects it onto another person. For example, a learner failing an exam might say, *"It wasn't my fault; it was because the teacher was incompetent."*, whereas in fact the real issue was their own unwillingness put enough effort. Some learners have such a big problem with projection that they completely deny their own agency and say things like, *"I'm behaving badly because you're not strict enough. You need to punish me more."*

In *regression*, an individual escapes anxieties in the here-and-now by reverting to an earlier point in their lives. For instance, a class of teenagers might respond to be asked to do something out of the ordinary by chaotically running around and making a lot of noise; they have regressed to being toddlers.

In *sublimation*, the individual re-channels the energy of unwanted impulses into an absorbing activity or creative effort of some sort. This can be quite useful; I have generally found that the most effective way of establishing some semblance of order in classes prone to toddler stage regression is to get them doing some sort of creative or problem-solving activity as quickly as possible.

In *repression,* the individual forces the memory of a traumatic event and/or its associated emotions out of consciousness.

In *disavowal*, the individual just refuses to acknowledge a fact which causes her anxiety. Paradoxically, she knows it but doesn't believe it.

In *reaction formation*, the individual expresses feelings that are the opposite of what his unconscious feels. He may, for example, display aggression towards someone for whom he unconsciously holds an infatuation.

In *transference*, the individual unconsciously relates to someone with whom they have a relationship in the present as if they were someone with whom they had a relationship in the past. For example, a male learner may relate to a female teacher as if she were his mother. Transference is often accompanied by *counter-transference* in which the object of transference unconsciously colludes with it, i.e. the female relates back to the male learner as if he were her son. Trying to discourage such phenomena will only strengthen them. It is far better (within the bounds of reason, common sense and what ethical standards will allow) to allow them to take their course, burning out naturally when they have served their psychological purpose.

I think that what is often behind some learners' failure to learn is an unconscious belief that they don't *deserve* to succeed. For others still, it may be a case of 'deep down inside' not really wanting to learn, of them only trying to do it to please others.

Because such unconscious influences are so powerful, teachers need to be willing to scratch below the surface sometimes and look for the learner's unconscious motivations. A person might, for instance, explain her decision to learn to drive in terms of wanting to have an easier commute to and from work. This is a perfectly valid reason and may be perfectly true to the person giving it at a conscious level. However, at a deeper level, she might be motivated by a desire for power and control, something she may open up about once she starts to feel a bond of trust developing between her and her teacher. At a deeper level still, she may be influenced by buried memories of feeling powerless and helpless as a small child. The teacher-learner relationship, like any meaningful relationship, can often develop by progressing through levels, starting with surface motivation but gradually going deeper and deeper as empathy increases. This can be of crucial importance because part of a teacher's role is to persuade a learner not to give up in the face of setbacks and she can only do this if she understands the learner's most powerful motivating factors.

Unconscious 'blocks' often become manifest in stressful conditions, for example when the exam candidate's mind 'goes blank', or when the driving test candidate's legs 'turn to jelly'. In both cases, the candidate is, in a sense, fighting against his own unconscious. Trying to defeat this invisible enemy through increased effort is futile because it just fights back stronger, but if the person calms down and relaxes, its power miraculously drains away. The key is to somehow instil *belief* in the mind of the learner; I could talk in great technical detail about what I'm doing when I'm driving a car but, in the end, the fundamental reason I can drive is that I *believe* that I can drive. The teacher's ability to get the learner to believe depends on the successful development between the two people of a transference/countertransference relationship which has emotional and unconscious elements as well as conscious and rational ones.

The psychoanalytic tradition, i.e. the belief that much of human behaviour can be explained with reference to the unconscious mind, clearly has much to offer education, but it has never been taken up with any enthusiasm by the state system in the U.K. There is, it seems, a collective disavowal of the evidence that the human mind is irrational, complex and paradoxical, and a tendency to cling steadfastly to banal cliches:

"They're lazy",

"They're not very bright",

"They don't really want to learn",

"They need a firm hand".

Unfortunately, many, if not all, teachers still want to live in a world of simple truths and black/white morality.

Britzman (2013) calls education 'the emancipatory project' and psychoanalysis 'the therapeutic project' and believes that both have at their centre a relationship (transference/counter-transference) through which issues of authority are played out. Moreover, both are concerned with making sense of experience through the construction of narratives. Members of the two professions *should* therefore regard themselves as natural allies and collaborators. Further weight to this argument comes from Awan (2017), who believes that teachers need to create space for learners to allow their natural instincts to come to the surface and find expression. He argues that, without allowing itself to acknowledge the existence of unconscious factors, education becomes a tug-of-war between a learner's instincts and the system's attempts to suppress them; for all the talk on the surface of care and nurturing, the reality underneath is one of brutality and coercion, rendering the learner increasingly neurotic as he progresses through the system.

The more I reflect on the lack of interest in psychoanalysis in the system, the more convinced I become that the real problem with it that its *emancipatory* potential is perceived as threatening and subversive. Part of the dynamic of how the state maintains its hold over people is that it presents itself as the Great Protector, a father figure, caring, yet able to be authoritarian when that is for the people's own good – Orwell's 'Big Brother'. What the state wants from the education system is not for it to produce individuals who question this narrative, but who readily buy into it – lots of law-abiding citizens who work hard and pay their taxes. For teachers to explore ideas which can potentially liberate people from the narrative and enable them to think for themselves is about as subversive as it gets.

At any given moment, an individual presents one particular version of himself to the outside world. However, this version may be just one of any number of versions of himself that he could have presented. A learner, for example, may present a version of himself that is self-critical and under-confident. This does not mean that another version of himself, a version that is highly confident and up for a challenge is not there lurking below the surface. It might simply be that he just wants to blend into the background and have an easy time. So, from a teacher's perspective, the question to be asked is, *"If this learner is presenting a low-confidence self to me, and if I suspect there is a more confident, more independent, self lurking below the surface, which version should I relate to?".* The conflict avoiding response, I think, would be to relate to what is being presented and to 'go easy' on the learner. But it might pay off sometimes to back your hunch that a more confident version of the person exists below the surface and to relate to *that* person instead. After all, this might be exactly what the learner actually wants at an unconscious level.

On the other hand, one might get a learner who presents a timid, vulnerable version of themselves because their strong, confident self doesn't really exist except perhaps in a faint, fragile form. If the teacher started pushing this learner out of his comfort zone, she would likely get a either a prickly or self-pitying response. I came across plenty of learners like this in adult basic skills education. Again, the easiest thing to do is to go easy on the learner. The problem with this, though, is that the learner just goes around in circles never getting anywhere. It also gives their unconscious the message that their teacher doesn't believe in them. On the other hand, if a robust, confident version of the person just isn't there, the 'throwing them in at the deep end' approach won't work either. An effective compromise approach I have often used successfully is to set learning challenges that are meaningful, but to break them down into small chunks, and to praise the learner enthusiastically as they meet these challenges. I also find it helpful, with this type of learner, to offer them a right of refusal: *"If you're not comfortable with something I ask you to do, just say so"*. By proceeding gently in this way, the teacher feeds and nurtures the emerging stronger self and, hopefully, this stronger self will eventually be able take on significant challenges with confidence.

Learning is essentially an interaction of conscious and unconscious, rational and emotional mental processes. Consider the following statement:

"I *love* English, but I *hate* maths."

Positive emotions such as love lead to positive motivation – the willingness to engage in an activity in the expectation that it will be enjoyable. Negative emotions, on the other hand, lead to the avoidance of an activity under the assumption that it will be unpleasant. As we have established, much of human emotion is kept locked away in the unconscious mind. In other words, people cannot always explain *why* they have positive feelings towards one thing but negative ones towards another and may become dumbstruck when asked to give such an explanation. Or, as we have seen, their conscious minds may invent bogus explanations so that they say what they *think* the reason is.

A huge amount of what we take in through our senses is outside the scope of what we give our conscious attention to; it simply seeps directly into our unconscious minds. Advertisers, who have known about this for decades, will use their understanding of the psychological mechanics of this to try to fly under the radar of consciousness and get directly to their target audience's unconscious minds. They know, for example, that people respond emotionally to sensory stimuli, particularly visual images, which have the power to trigger unconscious desires. These desires in turn create the motivation to buy products or, where such tactics are used in political contexts, to support causes.

How can we use our knowledge of this in teaching? One response might be: *"If the manipulation of unconscious processes can be used to sell cars, disinfectant, chocolate, political ideologies etc., why not use it to sell education as if it were simply another commodity?"*. I would caution against going down this road, however, on the grounds that it is cynically manipulative. If anything, I would argue, we should be raising learners' awareness of how advertisers and spin doctors manipulate them, not exposing them to more of the same.

If the brain can take in and process information subliminally, i.e. in a way that by-passes conscious awareness, it is just as well because the human capacity for focused attention is limited to short bursts. Imagine watching a movie. The chances are you will not maintain full conscious attention for the whole duration of the film. Instead, your attention will drift onto other matters, returning to the movie every so often. But this does not mean that you will reach the end of the movie and realise that you have no idea what it was about. This is because, while your conscious attention was wandering, relevant information from the movie was being absorbed and processed unconsciously.

In teaching people to drive, I generally find that learners can take in what I'm saying to them adequately enough as they're driving along whilst simultaneously paying attention to the road. Very occasionally, when I need to get across a crucial piece of information, I will get them to stop so that they can give me their full undivided attention. Conversely, if they need to give their full attention to the road, for example when they're judging when to emerge at a junction, I will not talk to them.

Conscious attention, it seems to me, is a special state of mind, a sort of trance state that we can enter into when the occasion demands it. It allows us to perform technical tasks cautiously and precisely, and giving an experience our conscious attention has a strange ability to intensify it. However, for much of the time we can function perfectly well without it. In fact, where it comes to education, the conscious mind's tendency to be questioning and suspicious, and to demand evidence before it believes anything, causes it to block the absorption of new ideas, especially if they seem unconventional or counter-intuitive. For this reason, subliminal perception can often succeed where conscious attention fails. This in fact is the principle on which hypnosis is based; the practitioner distracts the conscious mind by getting it to focus on an object or a repetitive activity, leaving the gateway to the trusting and suggestable unconscious mind unguarded. I often think that the best teachers are, probably without realising it, accomplished hypnotists, getting their most important messages – the ones to do with attitude and mindset – across indirectly through suggestion, insinuation and non-verbal communication whilst distracting their learners' conscious minds with something inconsequential. Incidentally, this skill of indirectly planting ideas in the unconscious minds of others also comes in useful in communicating with colleagues and authority figures in our employing organisations. To the accusation that this is being manipulative, I would reply that the unconscious will only accept suggestions it chooses to accept.

The unconscious mind responds better to pictures to words, but when words are used they will be more readily accepted if presented in short memorable phrases:

TAKE BACK CONTROL

GET BREXIT DONE

THINK FOR YOURSELVES

RESPECT OTHERS

TAKE RESPONSIBILITY

QUESTION AUTHORITY

I BELIEVE IN YOU

Note that the above phrases are all worded *positively*; there are no *"Do nots"*. Note also that the words *should* and *must* are not used at all.

The more a person is told they must do something, the less motivation they have to do it. This is because, by saying to someone, *"You must"*, we are indirectly giving their unconscious the suggestion that the thing they are required to do is not something they would choose to do of their own volition, so it must be something that is bad for them. People will only learn if they choose to learn and they will choose to learn if, and only if, the learning satisfies a perceived need. The following anecdote illustrates this point:

When I took up my VSO teaching post in Belize in 1998, I did so with the expectation that I would be mostly helping learners with basic literacy. To put it mildly, I was somewhat taken aback when I was subsequently asked to teach mathematics up to the equivalent of the U.K.'s GCSE level. The problem was that my own maths was atrocious. Up until that point, I had always assumed that I lacked the natural predisposition needed to be competent in the subject, seeing myself as creative and linguistic, but definitely not mathematical. But now I had a desperate need to be good at maths: if I couldn't do the job I was being asked to do, I would be sent back to the U.K. and have to deal with all the shame and embarrassment this would bring. This was unthinkable. So I went out, bought a textbook and studied it like my life depended on it. I made sure I got my maths up to a standard where I could teach it to secondary age pupils without difficulty. In reality, my problems with maths in the past had not stemmed from lack of ability but from lack of motivation based on a meaningful incentive.

It is all too easy to attribute lack of success to lack of ability when the real issue is motivation. I think that the significance of natural inequality – the fact that some people are more gifted than others – is grossly over-estimated and that the concept itself does more overall harm than good. What happens, I think, is that teachers develop opinions about particular learners' abilities that are often based on nothing more than negative stereotypes related to factors such as race, gender and social class. Teachers then, unwittingly perhaps, convey these opinions to learners by failing to reward their efforts with praise. This is massively important because the praise a learner gets from the teacher is his incentive to put in effort; it is what lies behind his motivation. Deprived of sufficient praise in response to effort, the learner concludes that effort is pointless, initiating a vicious circle where lack of praise and lack of effort simply reinforce each other. If this is initiated at the very beginning of a learner's formal education, by the time she reaches secondary school, the tendency for her to self-identify as a low achiever will have already become deeply ingrained. Conversely, learners on the receiving end of positive labelling will quickly self-identify as high achievers. This motivates them to work hard, leading to more success and praise, which motivates them to keep on working hard, and so the virtuous circle continues in perpetuity. A learner will tend to get into either one of these cycles early on in his progress through the system. I think that what makes all the difference is whether or not the learner has in her life someone, be it a teacher, family member or friend, who believes in them to such an extent that the positivity they get from this person counteracts the negativity they get from other quarters.

Discouragement can just as easily come from within the learner's own family or wider community as from her school. In her 2018 autobiography, Michelle Obama describes how, encouraged by her parents, she took easily to formal education. She enjoyed learning and quickly bought into the idea of education as opportunity. But one day, another kid in her community remarked to her, *"How come you talk like a white girl?* (p.40). The validity of the identity she had chosen for herself had been brought into question and the implied criticism, if it had been taken to heart, may have developed into a disincentive to engage in education. For Michelle, the incident caused her to stop and think, but no more than that. It didn't make her turn away from education, but it might have done had she not also had the more positive messaging coming from her family counteracting the negativity. It is not difficult to imagine how, for someone without this sort of encouragement, the emotional tug-of-war over the conflict between affirmation from her community and affirmation from school might lead to a different outcome.

The incident related by Michelle Obama highlights the fact that, for many, engaging in education entails choosing between two alternative versions of their own sense of self. Once a person has decided to reject formal education, only an inward change of heart can reverse it. Attempting to force such a change through disciplinarianism might lead to an outward change in behaviour in the short term, but it will only reinforce the underlying attitude.

A pro-education attitude is just as intransigent as an anti-education one. I was greatly moved when I read Malala Yousafzai's (2013) description of her childhood in Pakistan. Malala was, as a child, so passionate about her right to education that she continued to defy the Taliban and attend school in spite of the risk to her life that this entailed. Her courage led to her being shot in the head. If Malala's passion for education was so strong that even this experience could not shake it, then surely a few hours in detention would have little hope of obliterating the hatred of school harboured by someone who had decided to reject it.

Malala was fighting in a violent 'culture war' in which girls' education had become a symbol – loved by one side and hated by the other – but education can also be the battleground *for* culture wars. We often think of culture as something that brings people together, but it is often divisive and can become weaponized. If we take music as an example, by identifying strongly with a particular musical style, people are identifying with an associated sub-culture which sets itself up in opposition to the mainstream. The education system is usually viewed in this context as being part of the mainstream. Rather than conforming to the stereotype of the mainstream cultural authority figure and expressing disapproval of the sub-culture, a more imaginitive response on the part of the teacher might be to try and establish solidarity with the rebellious learners by accepting their sub-cultural identities. The teacher might then progress from this to try to get learners to channel their anti-establishment energies in a constructive direction.

I think that emotion, positive or negative, is a vital ingredient of any successful lesson. Without this, learners are apathetic, distant, cold – present in body but absent in spirit. If the teacher induces emotion, they drop their cynicism and open themselves up to new experience. There are various ways of doing this – pictures, music, film, humour, to name but four. These things are especially potent if they can be woven into a narrative because narrative plus emotion equals *drama*.

If we accept that we need learners to have positive feelings about the process of education itself, how can we get that to happen? Carl Rogers, in his classic text *Freedom to Learn* (1969), argues that, to properly engage learners at a personal and emotional level, teachers must be prepared to let go of their desire to initiate, control and evaluate the learning process. All this power should be handed over to the learners because only then does learning become truly meaningful to them. To threaten a learner's sense of self by being harsh or punitive will serve only to induce, and then reinforce, his emotional insecurity and feelings of inadequacy. The teacher should view herself as a facilitator rather than an authority figure, a member of the group with no greater status than anyone else rather than as an authority figure standing above it.

The ultimate aim of education is to produce human beings who have learnt how to learn, and can thus thrive in a world of constant change. The young people who were part of the great tidal wave of creativity that characterised the cultural landscape of the 1960s were doing just that. In fact, they weren't simply thriving on change, they were driving it. They came of age at a time when progressive, individualist ideas were in the ascendency and it was, I think, something about the amount of freedom and opportunity for self-expression they found themselves with that made all the difference. We need to somehow create these conditions within our present-day educational institutions, for all rather than a lucky few.

Though criticism is counter-productive, communicating to learners that you expect much from them because you believe in them is vital. Having the sort of classroom atmosphere described above does not mean always having a warm and cosy relationship with one's students. In fact, being too enamoured of warmth and cosiness is a dereliction of duty. Sometimes, we need to challenge them, rebuke them, push them into places they don't want to go, but we can only do this if we have earned the right, and we earn the right by building a relationship with them based on empathy, genuineness and acceptance.

There is a widespread assumption, I think, that what learners fear most is the prospect of failure. This is certainly true at the conscious level, but I suspect that, at a deeper level, the barrier to learning is fear of *transformation*. I would guess that, unconsciously, the fear of transformation is a fear of growing up, which is all about having to deal with reality and take responsibility. Earlier, we looked at Bettelheim's work on the significance of fairy tales for young children's emotional development and, if we consider the themes of these stories, we see that they generally tend to be about transformation of some sort. Adults too have an unconscious fear of transformation, but instead of having fairy tales read to them, they prefer to watch horror movies. Film critic Mary Campbell (2004) develops this idea by examining the work of the director David Cronenberg. The horror in a Cronenberg film, she suggests, stems from an uncomfortable feeling that things are getting out of control, that the pace of change is so fast that no-one can stop it. The viewer feels overwhelmed by it as boundaries that were previously distinct become increasingly blurred. These themes are wonderful metaphors, I think, for intellectual development and help us to understand resistance to it.

The psychoanalyst Donald Meltzer (1992) was also interested in the unconscious fear of change. In his view, every a time a person is confronted with something new it evokes the primal experience of the first encounter the infant has with the mother, provoking conflicting emotions of longing on the one hand and fear/aggression on the other. Psychologically, the experiencer oscillates between these two poles. This is the normal state of affairs, one of 'mental vitality', but some people retreat from this healthy state of conflict by symbolically taking refuge inside their mother's body. Thus, they cannot learn, grow or develop. The way out of this psychological prison ('claustrum') is through the lighting of an emotional fire inside the individual.

Another deeper level barrier to learning is the inverse to the one discussed above. This is the unconscious belief that formal education is powerless to bring about change. One of the stereotypes sometimes applied to working class people is that their culture is based on instant gratification, in contrast with middle class culture which is based on deferred gratification, and this is said to explain the supposed greater value attached by middle class people to formal education. If there is a kernel of truth to the stereotype, a likely reason is that working class people have historically understood that it will take much more than a few qualifications to open up for them the sorts of opportunities available to their middle class counterparts. It would in fact take nothing less than a fundamental re-structuring of society. If we go along with this pessimistic view, then the so-called deferred gratification promised by formal education is largely illusory and working class people might quite logically conclude that they might as well simply focus on instant gratification. Such an argument may no longer hold true in the way that it did in the past, and people may no longer buy into it at a conscious level, but attitudes of this kind are deeply engrained at the unconscious and cultural levels and tend to get passed down from generation to generation.

Of course, many working class people do see formal education as a way to escape their circumstances and will go along with the deferred gratification concept. It is also, I think, entirely plausible that any given learner may be unconsciously ambivalent towards the system. That is, part of him may view it as oppressive and as a waste of time, something to be kicked against, while another part of him may view it as an opportunity for a better life. Then there is the matter of guilt adding to the internalised drama: *"Do I deserve to better myself? Am I turning my back on where I came from?"*.

Once someone has bought into the deferred gratification concept and engages positively with the system, it can be difficult to get them to let go of it again. Personally, I hate the idea that there are thousands of students in universities up and down the country hating every minute of the course they are enrolled on, but telling themselves that they have to stick it out and somehow get through it because it will open the door to a lucrative career. It seems that people from working class backgrounds, painful memories of childhood poverty seared into their unconscious minds, are embracing the idea of education as a means of achieving their economic aspirations, but not as transformative in a greater sense.

Learning is a survival mechanism. It is biological in that it results in chemical, functional and structural changes in the brain. It could be said that, whereas the fight or flight response helps the organism deal with an immediate danger, learning is about becoming able to understand the environment in such a way as to control it and prevent the danger arising in the first place. However, the learning environment itself can be perceived by some individuals as threatening; it threatens the exposure of weaknesses and inadequacies and introduces the possibility of humiliating failure. When someone perceives a threat, their short-term survival strategy – their fight-or-flight response – kicks in, and it is not difficult to see how this response interferes with learning. If individuals are in the grip of powerful biological impulses in which the teacher becomes the equivalent of a wild beast and the classroom becomes the equivalent of a trap, no amount of reasoning will stop them either fighting the teacher or running away from him. I have vivid memories from the early years of my teaching career of yelling at groups of pupils: *"You're behaving like animals!"*. Of course they were! If the teacher responds by being fierce and threatening and turning the situation into a battle of wills which he, the teacher, ultimately wins, the likelihood then is that the pupil will adopt the strategy of 'playing dead' and withdraw from engagement altogether. This state of affairs could quite conceivably drag on for years, until the pupil is finally released from the prison.

As well as recognising the fight-or-flight response in learners, I think that a teacher needs to recognise that he too will produce such a response when he feels threatened. When it happens, it will come across in non-verbal communication (facial expression, tone of voice, posture) and will only exacerbate the learners' own fight-or-flight response. If the teacher develops enough self-awareness to realise when this is happening, he can then try to self-talk his way to a calmer state.

Motivation is tightly intertwined with the notion of *meaning;* what, if anything, does a particular area of knowledge *mean* to the learner? In Chapter 3, we encountered the fictional character of Billy Casper who, mostly through his own imagination, but encouraged also by a wonderful teacher, was able to construct an alternative narrative about himself as a skilled trainer of birds of prey. For Billy, the formal curriculum he was having imposed on him at school meant nothing, but his self-taught skill in falconry meant freedom, being in control, feeling fully alive. The brilliance of his English teacher, Mr. Farthing, was in recognising this and finding a way to get Billy to forge a link in his mind between his English lessons and his great passion. Mr. Farthing understood both the connection between motivation and learning and that between meaning and motivation.

The 'problem pupils' we see at secondary school and in Further Education are the products of a gradual process of demotivation which began during their earliest days in school. In order to stand even a chance of helping them, we need to make an imaginative leap and get inside the mind of a five year-old child on his first day at school. Here, he experiences a nightmarish world of confusing rituals and incomprehensible rules which induce a feeling of imprisonment and a yearning to escape which only intensifies as the years progress. For protection, he builds a wall of apathy and insolence around himself.

My own school career could so easily have gone that way. The first school I attended as a small child was visible from the window of our home. Before I even went there, I would gaze at the place longingly, eagerly anticipating my first day. School, after all, was where they taught you to read, and I loved stories. How amazing it would be, I thought, to be able to read them for myself! Then I started school and, sure enough, I learnt to read. But there was something else, something I hadn't been expecting; I got shouted at a lot. I got shouted at for hanging my coat on the wrong peg, for sitting at the wrong table, for wearing the wrong footwear, for looking out of the window. In fact, it seemed to me at the time that I could get shouted at for just about anything at any time. In addition to learning to read and write and add and subtract etc., I was learning to fear authority and to know my place. But I had a secret weapon: my imagination. This enabled me to escape much of the conditioning by taking refuge in my own fantasy world, a world where I could be anyone I wanted to be and do anything I wanted. Fortunately, there were also one or two teachers who understood me and gave me encouragement rather than criticism. The upshot was that I ultimately emerged from my years of schooling with my self-confidence somewhat dented, but with my ability to think for myself and use my imagination largely intact. I was one of the lucky ones.

Successful people often look back on their lives and think to themselves, *"Things could have gone very differently, but there was this one teacher who believed in me, and that's what made all the difference"*. If I could give someone starting out in teaching one piece of advice it would be this: be that one teacher who made a difference.

Billy Casper, like me, was not a lost cause. He was capable all along of responding positively to a teacher with just the right blend of sensitivity and know-how. It has to be said that not all reluctant learners are salvageable. Some are so badly damaged that they resist all attempts at empathy. They give the impression that they get a perverse pleasure from being as disruptive as possible to other people's right to learn. I have experienced my fair share of this in my teaching career. I have tried to engage with such individuals in an attempt to understand their motivation from their own perspective but have had little success. A feature of their underlying attitude is a refusal to articulate their true thought and feelings, something like the mafia code of *omerta*. My educated guess, from observing them, is that being destructive gives them a feeling of power, and, if they do it publicly and direct it towards an authority figure, they are rewarded with high status within their social group.

How does one deal with this at a practical level? The secondary school I taught at in Belize had a number of individuals of this kind in its student body. They were relatively small in number but there were enough of them to cause major disruption. Some of them were involved in gang culture and drug-dealing outside school and brought that into the school environment. Others were interested in sexually harassing female students. One way of inadvertently rewarding disruptive behaviour, thereby making it worse, is to become embroiled in dramatic confrontations with individuals. The individual in question, we have to remember, is playing to his own audience. Above all, the teacher cannot let himself be provoked into doing or saying something in the heat of the moment that would allow the disrupter to adopt the moral high ground. Generally speaking, for a teacher to display a certain amount of emotion is a good thing as it shows authenticity but, when one is dealing with the worst kinds of disruptive behaviour, *sangfroid* is often called for

Beneath the veneer of civilised behaviour, a human being is just another animal with animalistic needs, instincts and impulses. An adult choosing to engage in education with a clear purpose in mind has much more of an incentive to keep these things in check than a child or adolescent undergoing compulsory education. Such reluctant conscripts can, at times, quite literally find it impossible to keep still. The human animal is built for *action* triggered by emotions and instincts. It takes self-discipline on the part an individual to be able to over-rule his animal nature. This raises the question of how to help a learner develop self-discipline. Some learners may *seem* to respond very well to the sergeant major approach in which harsh discipline imposed by an authority figure eventually gets internalised and becomes self-discipline. However, I am not a supporter of such an approach.

The reason why, I think, disciplinarianism seems to work with some individuals is that such people have an unconscious fear of taking responsibility for their own behaviour and therefore unconsciously long to be told what to do. But our task as teachers is not to pander to this fear of freedom by adopting a disciplinarian mindset – that would do nothing to help learners overcome it. Nor is it to try to confront the fear by removing any semblance of order and structure and forcing learners to take responsibility – we have seen that trying to fight an unconscious impulse only serves to strengthen it and the learners will respond by behaving more and more obnoxiously until the teacher has no option but to enforce discipline. Rather, our job is to patiently and empathically explore the underlying fear in an environment where learners feel emotionally secure enough to lower their defences.

Resistance to authority is psychologically healthy and synonymous with being creative and we should not interfere with that too much. In the U.K. in the 1950s, there was a system of compulsory national service for young men in which they were temporarily enlisted in the military and subjected to military style discipline, complete with terror-inducing sergeant majors. In 1960, national service was abolished and the next generation of 'ill-disciplined' young men did not have this experience. What many of them did instead was become creative in fields such as music, painting, photography and cinema – careers that both require and help to develop strong self-discipline. I wonder what would have happened to them if they had been forced to do national service and had had the rebelliousness knocked out of them? What cultural achievements might the world have missed out on?

People often have a very simplistic view of how the world works and therefore have a tendency to look for simple solutions to complex questions. One of the purposes of education, I think, is to provide an antidote to this, to point out the complexities of life as well as to encourage people to look for solutions by thinking through those complexities, not to avoid thinking by putting problems into simple categories. The easy way to deal with something you don't understand is to stick a label on it; the hard way is to think your way through to an understanding of it. I would add the caveat that, If professional educators see themselves as having the task of instilling this attitude in others, they need also to instil it in themselves.

Military-style disciplinarianism is a strategy based on the deliberate induction of anxiety – for everyone, including the teachers who have to enforce it. Anxiety, as I understand it, is a profound feeling of not being in control which can, at its worst, tear people apart psychologically. Where it is used as a deliberate strategy to enforce conformity, it works by making people feel that they are being monitored all the time, and that the slightest rule violation will have terrible consequences. I would argue that, in the longer term, the approach alienates the Billy Caspers in the system and screws up their life chances in the process. And there are a lot of them. In 2019, almost one-in-five U.K. school leavers left with less than five GCSEs (Guardian, 20/09/2019).

Think of the consequences of this for national economic productivity. The fact that the U.K. has high performing elites can all too easily obscure the truth, namely that, for the great bulk of the population, productivity is alarmingly low. Of all the G7 nations, only Italy has shown a lower rate of improvement in productivity since 2007 (source: National Office of Statistics). We have a highly unequal society, the stark reality of which is reflected in low living standards for working class -people, and it was all too easy to scapegoat immigrants who came in to fill the skills gap. Back in 1969, Billy could have got a manual labour job, in coal mining or in some other form of heavy industry. Strange as it may sound, he was relatively lucky; his modern day counterparts face the more depressing prospect of low-paid and insecure zero-hours contract work. The answer, according to many economists, is to invest in hi-tec industries which provide high-pay employment, but the lack of a suitable educated workforce deters such investment.

But the consequences of the authoritarian style of education go beyond mere economics; it can also have a severely detrimental effect on the individual's ability simply to form healthy relationships and be happy. As someone who worked in a prison for twelve years, it is my opinion that individuals so affected have a greater chance of ending up in the criminal justice system. A huge proportion of the prisoners I met had stopped going to school on a regular basis long before they had reached the legal leaving age; what was it about it that they hated so much?

The science of psychology has allowed us to move beyond control through the induction of anxiety, with its long-term risks of causing neurosis, to what might be seen as more enlightened methods. Some of these methods involve an implicit medicalisation of undesired behaviour. Here, the learner behaving undesirably is viewed as having a psychological disorder, for example 'Attention Deficit Hyperactivity Disorder' (ADHD) or 'Oppositional Defiant Disorder'. Once the correct disorder has been diagnosed, an appropriate course of treatment can be prescribed. The drug Ritalin, for example, is commonly used to treat ADHD, whilst other types of behavioural disorder might be treated using various forms of 'behaviour therapy'.

In prisons, discipline amongst inmates is maintained not by overt disciplinarianism (the induction of anxiety) but by a system of rewards and incentives. For example, good behaviour will result in more visits, more phone calls and things like in-cell TV. The prisoners themselves are assumed to be rational beings who will, given the opportunity, choose the course of action that best serves their interests. Can such an approach be replicated in a non-custodial setting? There is no reason why not. First, the teacher would establish a voluntary principle by saying to disruptors, *"I don't care whether you do the work or not, just don't disrupt others".* Second, he could introduce elements of a reward/sanction system, ensuring in the process that the system was easily understood and that he was consistent and predictable in applying it. What precise rewards and sanctions are utilised would depend on what powers the teacher had and would vary from context to context, but the crucial thing is allowing the learner to make the choice for themselves based on their understanding of the consequences.

Such a scientific approach is indeed an improvement on control through the induction of anxiety, but it is still control, still a form of manipulation. Most prisoners do toe the line when they are in prison, but that is not necessarily the case when they are released from the controlling regime and are free to choose for themselves how to behave in the wider community. In fact, the prison regime may actually be counter-productive as it is *too* structured, thus rendering those released less capable of coping with the chaotic nature of life outside than when they went in. The same could be said of discharged armed forces personnel and of pupils leaving school. People who have become *institutionalised* in this way can only really function in environments where the emphasis is on rigid rules and routines rather than on independence and coping with the unpredictable; a person can only learn to be free by experiencing freedom.

Just after I left prison education, I worked as a supply teacher in state secondary schools. I was struck not by the differences between the two environments but by their *similarities* – the emphasis in both types of institution on regimentation, on keeping 'inmates' busy, and on monitoring their behaviour. Those schools which prided themselves most on their high levels of discipline achieved this through levels of policing and surveillance that would put a totalitarian state to shame. Do we honestly believe that this is the way to develop human potential, to produce mentally healthy adults capable of responding creatively to life's challenges? Foucault (1975) argues that, whilst the institutions of modern industrial states – schools, prisons, mental hospitals, factories and so on – might be superficially different to one another, their underlying purpose is always *control*, on replacing the traditional tyranny of physical violence with a new tyranny of order and routine.

For A.S. Neil in the 1920s, the solution to the ill-effects of the authoritarian model of education was not the adoption of more scientific methods of control but to create an environment where learners were free to choose for themselves to what extent they would engage in formal learning activities. To this end, he founded a school in which staff and pupils had equal status and equal decision-making power, a project he wrote about in his book *Summerhill: A Radical Approach to Child-Rearing* (1960). But children who get to go to an independent school already have a massive unfair advantage. Surely the real challenge is not to provide an alternative type of education for the lucky few whose parents have the means to buy them one, but to transform the state system from within and turn it into an environment where people can learn to be free? This is, in my view, achievable but it is going to take a heavy dose of pragmatism and some clever strategic thinking.

I have already discussed humour in relation to creativity. I now wish to discuss its role as a catalyst in the development of teacher-learner relationships and as an antidote to tension, stress and anxiety. Building relationships with learners is a hit-and-miss affair. The psychanalytical concepts of transference and counter-transference can help us to understand what is going on at an unconscious level, but I always think that the litmus test of a good relationship is whether or not the two people can make each other laugh; your sense of humour can often be your way in. There are lots of ways of making another person laugh, but I usually get my biggest laughs when I simply speak the truth. This is because, when someone speaks the truth in a situation where the cultural norm is for to be polite and hide what you really feel, people instinctively laugh because they are letting go of tension. It is as if they have suddenly been given permission to put down a heavy burden that they've been carrying for what feels like an eternity. You do, of course, need to know your audience; going close to the edge produces laughter, going over it causes embarrassment and an increase in tension.

I have played the humour card over and over again in my teaching career, especially when I have felt the need to develop a more relaxed relationship with a learner or group of learners. I suppose that the evolution process I've undergone in the way I think about teaching over the years has been one away from viewing it as being primarily an attempt to directly get learners to meet learning objectives towards viewing it as an attempt to get them to drop their psychological defences just enough to open themselves up to a transformative experience.

In general, being watched and judged has a harmful effect on a person's performance level on any given task. It just makes them try too hard, ratchets up the tension; the conscious mind is trying to do something which is usually left to the much more competent unconscious mind. The mind narrows its field of perception, limiting its ability to take in new information. For the unfortunate learner in this state, time itself seems to speed up so she has that panicky sense of lots of things happening to her in all at once and of not having enough time to process the information, let alone decide what to do. The learner can all too easily find herself in a negative feedback loop whereby anxiety leads to poor performance which in turn leads to more anxiety, leading to worse performance, and so on.

When a teacher becomes aware that a learner is caught in this trap, she clearly needs to communicate empathy, warmth, patience, kindness and humour. But is this really all we can do? Anxiety is caused not by the objective realities of a given situation but by its *interpretation* – the story the person tells himself about the situation causing the anxiety. Cognitive behavioural therapy (CBT) is a therapeutic approach which aims to get individuals to verbally reinterpret situations and question underlying assumptions in such a way that anxiety is diminished. I think of it as the left side of the brain acting as a counsellor to the right side. I am of the view that teachers would be much more effective at helping learners overcome anxiety if they were at least familiar with the principles of CBT. One version of it is Ellis's (1976) 'Rational-Emotive Behaviour Therapy', which postulates that people carry around with them basic beliefs about reality and that some of these beliefs are both wrong and self-destructive. These could include, for example, a belief that they must constantly achieve perfection, or a belief that they must always be approved of by others. In the educational context, these sorts of distorted versions of reality can lead to the magnification of the importance of small errors and the minimisation of the significance of successes. I also think that it is quite common for learners being assessed to believe that it is their worth *as a person* that is being judged, as opposed to their performance on a task. Another common false assumption is that they only have one chance to succeed so failure is final. All these irrational beliefs can make an individual want to run away from a challenge rather than take it on. The teacher should aim to confront such thoughts and help learners replace them with more realistic ones, then to encourage them to go towards the challenge rather than away from it.

CBT is a sort of damage repair strategy. It would be far better if the damage, namely, the fear of failure, wasn't sustained in the first place. The best way to inoculate against performance anxiety is by instilling confidence at an early age. Confidence, in the sense that I am using the word here, is the ultimate antidote to all the psychological barriers hitherto discussed and arises through the individual experiencing unconditional love.

I believe that bad schooling experiences can stunt the development of healthy self-belief, even for those from loving backgrounds. It is often said that confidence is one of the advantages a private education gives a person over their equally talented state-educated counterpart. I think that the key to having an education system which instils confidence is to convey high expectations whilst simultaneously giving learners the message that failure does not diminish the positive regard felt for them. If we have the former without the latter, we are setting them up for a pattern of failure and this leads to self-loathing, the basis of future performance anxiety issues.

When teaching people who are very low in confidence, it can often be useful to give them an early experience of success, even if it has to be manufactured. This gives the learner the sense that they *can* learn and can kick start a learning journey. But if this approach is pursued for too long it can create a deluded learner. I feel strongly that it is vital to move learners on to genuine challenges, challenges where there is a real chance of failure, as soon as the initial confidence has been established. the trouble with the confidence-building theory if pursued for too long is that, although the learner's conscious mind might be fooled, their unconscious mind sees through the deception so that what you end up with is a flimsy, unsustainable sort of confidence, something that will evaporate the moment it is tested.

Unearned confidence can be a dangerous thing. Dunning and Kruger (1999) discovered that the more incompetent a person was at a particular skill, the more he tended to over-estimate his abilities; the lower a person's level of competence, the less insight he has into what he's doing wrong and the more blissfully unaware he is of how incompetent he is. There are times when we need to attack and destroy the wrong sort of confidence before rebuilding the learner with the right sort.

Teachers are prone to the same unconscious biases and prejudices that affect all human beings. Rosenthal and Jacobson (1968) studied the effects of teacher expectations on academic attainment. They told teachers in a California elementary school that some of their students were especially gifted. In fact, the names were simply chosen at random. Those students who had been identified as being gifted subsequently improved their average grades. Somehow or other, the teachers had communicated high expectations to those learners they believed were gifted, and the learners had somehow or other picked up on this and adjusted their behaviour accordingly. This may help to explain racial and gender differences in achievement – teachers are affected by unconciously-held stereotypes.

Good (1987) describes two distinct mechanisms through which teacher low expectations can adversely affect learner achievement. The first is the 'self-fulfilling prophecy effect' in which learners labelled as low-achievers will adjust their behaviour is response to the label and consequently go on to become low-achievers. It is this effect that the Rosenthal and Jacobson study so clearly exposes. The second is the 'sustaining expectation effect' in which it is assumed that learners who are observed to be exhibiting in the present behavioural characteristics considered unconducive to high academic achievement will go on exhibiting the same characteristics in the future. The underlying belief which gives rise to this effect can be summed up in the old proverb, *"A leopard can't change its spots."* In reality, however, people often do change as they mature and it is a shame when an individual who has transformed himself continues to suffer as a consequence of the way he behaved in the past.

The expectations teachers have of learners often arise from objectively administered initial assessment tests. Such tests, if designed in such a way that they eliminate cultural bias, *can* be a force for good. Their great value, potentially, is that they enable the provision of individualised learning programmes through which the relatively less able are given relatively more support. But the problem arises when such tests are used to predict *ultimate* outcomes and where such predictions are used to limit opportunity. This is where both the self-fulfilling prophecy effect and the sustained expectation effect can come into play.

Low expectations can also can have a devastating effect when applied more generally, perhaps to whole institutions, or to whole groups in society, where there has been a history of low achievement. What low expectations tend to lead to in such contexts is a belief that the only way to improve achievement is to lower standards.

Rather than either lowering standards or over-supporting learners, we need to use authentic ways of improving achievement. One such way is to work to enhance the learners' psychological resilience, to help them to become better at coping with setbacks, fighters rather than runners. An individual who habitually responds to failure by interpreting it as evidence that she will never succeed needs to change the way she understands failure. Syed (2015) argues that too many people labour under the misapprehension that failure is a bad thing. On the contrary, he asserts, failure is a stage on the road to ultimate success. If a learner has a self-defeating understanding of failure, it falls upon the teacher to help him to reframe the understanding, and one of the most effective ways of doing this is to cite examples of individuals from the world of celebrity who have drawn strength from failure and then gone on to find huge success. This quote from soccer coach Marcello Bielsa is telling:

"Being successful deforms us as human beings, it relaxes us, it plays tricks on us, it makes us worse individuals, it helps us fall in love with ourselves. Failure is the complete opposite, it forms us, it makes us more solid, it brings us closer to our convictions, it makes us more coherent."

In a similar vein, here's one from basketball legend Michael Jordan:

"I've missed more than 9000 shots in my career. I've lost almost 300 games. 26 times, I've been trusted to take the game winning shot and missed. I've failed over and over and over again in my life. And that is why I succeed."

And look at this one from the poet Maya Anjelou:

"Courage allows the successful woman to fail and learn powerful lessons from the failure. So that in the end, she didn't fail at all."

Powerful stuff; the wider culture is there as a free resource to be used.

The learner needs to understand that failure is a golden opportunity to learn, but he also needs to be given the freedom to come up with his own creative responses to failure rather than having remedies thrust upon him; *"I have concluded that I must work harder."* is better than *"My teacher has told me I need to work harder."*

Failure is a psychological trauma and how successfully a person deals with a trauma has a great deal to do with the number and severity of traumas they have had to deal with in the past. A person from a disadvantaged background is likely to have had to deal with several traumas already, perhaps some severe ones, before they even present themselves to you in your classroom. In such a case, you cannot glibly tell them that they need to develop a different attitude and expect them to absorb the advice without any problem. You must first work hard to build a relationship with that person, to win their trust. That way, you earn the right to advise them about their attitude.

There are some abilities that virtually all human beings come into the world already able to do. It is said, for example, that if you throw a baby into a swimming pool this will activate a reflex which will make it swim, or at least float without inhaling water. There are other abilities which only a tiny minority will ever be able to do, for example having perfect musical pitch or the potential to run the 100 metres in under ten seconds. In between these two extremes are abilities that are neither natural instincts that come easily nor rare talents possessed by a few, but *skills* that can be learnt. Driving would be a good example, but so too would be mastery of the subjects on an academic curriculum. These sorts of skills are within the grasp of the vast majority of people provided they are prepared to put themselves through the learning process. And putting oneself through a learning process means experiencing failure. I would go as far as to say that the prime determining factor in whether a person ultimately succeeds at learning a new skill is their ability to keep bouncing back from failure.

I was once working with a group of female learners in adult education. Some of these women, I think, were suffering from the phenomenon known as 'learned helplessness' in which repeated experiences of trying yet failing to improve their lives through their own efforts had taught them that trying was a waste of energy, that they might as well just wait for someone to help them. They wanted me to give them so much help that I would have been virtually doing the work for them, but I instead chose to challenge them – to insist that they tried harder to work more independently. It worked, but it might not have. I had chosen the riskier option. A teacher needs to be prepared to take calculated risks rather than always taking the safer option. Sometimes, teaching is just pushing someone off a cliff when they're not expecting it.

People with disabilities, be they visible or invisible, physical or psychological, and people who are disadvantaged in other ways, need to push themselves harder than the average person to achieve success. This is simply a statement of fact. Their teachers would be letting them down if they didn't encourage them to push themselves hard, but push themselves hard in areas that were *meaningful to them*, and with an underlying message of *"I believe in you"*.

Allowing learners to find their own meanings and motivations rather than imposing yours on them is of the utmost importance. The wheelchair basketball star turned television presenter, Ade Adepitan, gave an interview to *The Telegraph's* Tom Ough in 2018 in which he described his route to success. Born in Nigeria, Ade was afflicted with polio as a young child and was left physically disabled. At the age of three, his family moved to London, where he had to deal with all the challenges of being a foreigner in a strange land on top of those posed by his disability. Ade found meaning in his situation in his love of sport which made him physically stronger and more independent. He was able to walk with callipers, but chose to use a wheelchair. He hints that his father disapproved of this, preferring that he kept using the callipers. Perhaps his father felt that persevering with the callipers represented a triumph over the disability and an assertion of his son's normality, but for Ade the wheelchair offered the promise of greater independence. For him, it was the independence that was the driving force, the thing that gave his efforts meaning, not the appearance of normality.

In some cases, the barrier to learning is not the fear of failure but the fear of letting go of what is familiar, of getting used to new things, whether they are new behaviour patterns or new ways of thinking. This 'getting used to' process requires patient, dogged determination. Some learners have this quality in abundance but others need to be coached to find it within themselves. Otherwise, they are in danger of simply giving up. The 'getting used to things' phenomenon is universal. I once had a conversation with one of my driving pupils about her reluctance to go above 20mph. We talked about de-sensitisation, the process by which something new becomes less and less anxiety-inducing as you become used to it. She told me that her two-year-old daughter was beginning to understand the concept of 'getting used to things' in the context of all the challenges she was facing in her infant life. The difference between her and her daughter was that, for the daughter, giving up was not an option.

Dealing with people who have a tendency to want to quit when the going gets tough is one thing, but the ones who never properly engage in the first place are a whole different level of challenge. In my driving instruction work, I occasionally come across learners who have lesson after lesson over a long period of time but fail to make any significant progress, despite my best efforts. These tend to be people who will not engage with what I'm trying to teach them and who give the impression of not thinking about driving at all in the time between lessons. It is as if they have the expectation that just being there ought to be enough for them to learn –

remember the barber's chair analogy from Chapter 1. Of course, just being there is never enough;the learner needs to be present emotionally as well, to be fully committed.

Gladwell (2008) describes what he calls the '10,000 hour rule'; it takes 10,000 hours of practice, he says, to master any given skill. Putting 10,000 hours in requires the learner to work on their own away from the classroom environment and it takes self-discipline, lots of it. If a learner fails to achieve because they lack this, then this is hardly the teacher's fault. The learner needs to ask himself, *"How much do I really want this?"*.

Of course, personal effort is not the only factor that determines whether a person becomes successful or not; many other variables are involved. For Gladwell, luck plays a big part. The luck involved might be genetic, cultural, economic, or simply circumstantial, but I would argue that educational luck can be hugely significant also. By educational luck, I mean having the good fortune to come across the right teacher at the right time. By being the best teacher one can possibly be, one is increasing the likelihood that one will become, for any given learner, that right teacher at the right time. Now, what 'the right teacher at the right time' looks like will vary from learner to learner. While, for one learner, it might be a strict parental figure who keeps them on the straight and narrow, for another it might be the first person in their whole life who treats them as an adult. This is where, I think, a teacher needs to have the wisdom to be her authentic self and not try to be all things to all learners, and, hardest of all, to accept that, sometimes, they are going to be the wrong teacher at the wrong time.

Chapter 6

The Emancipatory Project

Teachers will sometimes talk about 'empowerment', in accordance with the old adage that 'knowledge is power'. But a commitment to empowerment in the classroom is meaningless unless accompanied by a willingness to acknowledge the institutional and socio-economic inequalities that lie behind oppression.

When I worked in offender learning between 2002 and 2014, the contract to deliver education in my prison was put out to competitive tender. As a consequence, I worked for an employer which saw people at the very bottom of society as a resource to be exploited for financial gain. They were simply taking advantage of a system set up by the government with the aim of getting the best value for money for tax-payers. As teachers, do we ignore this wider context and concentrate simply on relating to learners in the classroom, or do we somehow try to engage with it?

Here is another example. When I worked as a VSO volunteer in Belize, I was a white person struggling to teach learners whose ancestors had been exploited by white people for centuries and who were only too aware of their poverty powerlessness in relation to white people. This was a powerlessness that education alone could do little to resolve as it was rooted in complex economic structures that were fundamentally unfair. Again, can a teacher simply ignore the wider context and say, *"Nothing to do with me."*?

If we really want education to be about empowerment, we need to face up to these sorts of realities and do what we can to change them. That means being prepared to address them with learners in such a way that they are inspired to take action, to challenge the systems of oppression which hold them down.

Am I a Marxist? This is a question I have often asked myself. My efforts to answer it are not helped by the fact that there isn't just one type of Marxism but several. There are Trotskyists, Stalinists, Maoists, humanist Marxists, structural Marxists, instrumentalist Marxists, neo-Marxists and un-reconstructed Marxists, to name but a few. I'm an individualist first and foremost and I certainly feel no great affinity with Marxist activists as a group, tending to find them humourless and unimaginative. Some of them come across as having been brainwashed. They claim to be on the side of working class people, but seem more attracted to the idea of imposing change from the top rather than allowing it to grow organically from the bottom. This suggests they have a very low estimation of what working class people can achieve without authoritarian leadership. I have often felt uncomfortable, bullied even, in their presence.

Having said that, social inequality, and the extent to which education can either reinforce or undermine it, is a subject close to my heart. Clearly, all institutions exert power and, in formal education, power/resistance relationships are a constant and inescapable fact. The first question we need to ask is, *"Can resistance ever be legitimate in formal educational settings?"* My answer to that question is a straightforward 'Yes', and this has profound consequences for how I relate to learners. If this makes me a sort of Marxist, so be it.

Steele and Taylor (2004) provide an historical analysis of the influence of Marxism on Further and Adult Education in the UK. They paint a picture of the persistence of a Marxist tradition competing with a more mainstream tradition emphasising functionally useful knowledge and skills. Ruskin College in Oxford, for example, was at the forefront of Marxist working class education in the early years of the 20th century. However, when I taught there between early 2015 and late 2016, I got the impression that its radical tradition existed primarily as a veneer. Some of the teachers were keen to promote radical ideas, but they were in a minority and the management's overriding priority seemed to be to maximise state funding, largely by implementing a curriculum the state approved of. Contrast this to 1909 when the then Principal, Dennis Hird, supported the students when they went on strike to demand a more Marxist curriculum! Ruskin, when I taught there, still catered for disadvantaged learners, and was rightly proud of the fact, but that is not the same thing as offering them a radical education and challenging oppression. If this sort of management is the prevailing orthodoxy in formal education in our present age, the onus is surely on the teacher in the classroom to take the lead in creating a soil where radical ideas can take root and flourish.

I think, however, that the real relevance of Marxism in education does not lie in the explicit teaching of Marxist theories, but from its potential to assist in developing an approach to teaching that seeks solidarity with learners who come from oppressed sections of society, rather than seeking to control them. The starting point has to be the development of empathy with the subjective experience of the learner and an unconditional acceptance of the validity of such experience. If a teacher can do this, she is communicating the idea of equality *indirectly* – communicating with the unconscious minds of her learners. It might be said that, though she may not be teaching politics, she is teaching *politically*.

Barack Obama, in his autobiographical *Dreams From My Father* (1995), describes his experiences of being a 'Community Organiser' as a young man in Chicago. Part of his role was to try to motivate members of (mostly black) disadvantaged communities to become politically engaged. It could be said that he was trying to create a sort of counterculture, or at least to revive one that already existed but which was in danger of fading away. At first, he was unsuccessful, but things improved when he began to realise that he couldn't separate political motivation from the individual life stories of the people he was trying to motivate. He speaks of *"...the wall I had erected between psychology and politics"* (p.194). Obama is, of course, writing from the point of view of a politician who comes to realise that he needs to understand something about human psychology, something that people of the hard left never quite seem to learn. I think, though, that a parallel can be drawn between what Obama was trying to do and the work of teachers who aspire to be make a difference, for we too are in danger of building barriers between the psychological and the political. Whereas for Obama his problem was that he was giving so much attention to the political that he ignored the psychological, for teachers it is the reverse; in focusing solely on relationships with learners as individuals, they neglect the need to raise political consciousness.

Critical Pedagogy (Abraham, 2014) proposes that education should aim to develop in the mind of the learner 'critical consciousness' – consciousness, that is, of the social and cultural context in which she lives and her relationship with it. From this perspective, education should quite explicitly aspire to transform society, to make the world fairer and more equal. Critical Pedagogy is, in essence, a way of thinking about education that completely rejects the notion that a teacher can, or should try to be, *apolitical.* It rests on the hope that it is possible to transform society from the bottom up, by transforming the consciousness of individuals. In trying to make this hope a reality, it places the teacher/learner relationship at the heart of education and proposes that this relationship should be based on compassion and shared goals. It requires teachers to be an 'intellectuals', not in the elitist sense but in the sense of reflecting seriously upon the political implications of their work (more on this in Chapter 10). Crucially, such teachers are expected to pass on this way of thinking to their learners so that they in turn become social critics and social transformers.

Two key figures in the development of Critical Pedagogy are the psychoanalyst Erich Fromm (1942) and the educationalist Paulo Freire (1970, 1974, 1998). Both theorists see the education process as one of breaking free from oppression. This liberation process involves overcoming what Fromm calls 'the fear of freedom' – the tendency of oppressed peoples to *internalise oppression,* that is to adopt for themselves, uncritically, the logic of their oppressors, thereby doing the work of oppression for them. If people are freed from external oppression whilst the internal chains remain intact, they will, Fromm believes, respond in one or more of three ways: by submitting to an authoritarian leader, by becoming oppressors themselves, or by adopting a behaviour pattern of mindless conformity. In viewing education as liberation from internalised oppression, we see once again a close parallel between education and psychoanalysis (see previous chapter). Just like the patient in psychoanalysis, the learner going through education cannot achieve liberation through his own efforts alone, only in the context of a relationship with another, in this case the teacher.

For oppressed individuals, their many particular experiences of oppression become fused into one and, together, incubate a deep sense of frustration whose causes they cannot necessarily articulate in rational terms, but which find their voice in anger and aggression. As teachers, we may come face to face with this in our everyday work. Rather than listening to this voice and trying to understand it, teachers tend to classify the phenomenon under the heading of 'challenging behaviour', certain in the assumption that it is both non-legitimate and undesirable, and seek to combat it by re-asserting control. By doing this, they, inadvertently perhaps, become oppressors themselves.

It would be neglectful to discuss the role of education in challenging oppression without considering the issue of gender. Germaine Greer (1971) advocates that women should rebel against the identities imposed on them by men – identities of intellectual inferiority, passivity and sexual objectification. During my time in prison education, I taught convicted rapists. It is all very well doing therapy and rehabilitation when the damage has already been done, but I cannot help wondering whether a deep and serious exploration of power issues around gender with school-aged males might contribute to the prevention of the development of the sorts of misogynistic attitudes that see their most extreme manifestations in sex crimes against women.

I have also worked with women who were juggling the requirements of academic learning with the demands on them to conform to the stereotype of care-giving in the family. In most cases, such was their determination to make their lives better that they pressed on with their studies, often succeeding against the odds. I think that it is important for teachers to acknowledge when learners are carrying extra baggage like this and to turn the classroom into a safe haven where these issues can be explored in depth. At the same time, I think that it would be a betrayal to give learners an easy time because of such issues.

Critical pedagogy implies that the teacher/learner relationship should essentially be a partnership. One way of attempting to put this principle into practice is through 'learner-led education' (LED) and this approach was the subject of a research study conducted by Iverson et al (2015). The data the researchers collected, all of it gathered in a Higher Education context, consisted of teaching plans, interviews with teachers and learners, questionnaires and surveys of learners, and individual student portfolios. The report on the project speaks of learners and teachers 'co-creating' the learning process. Learners, under teacher guidance, decide for themselves what questions are important to them and how these questions should be investigated. LED encompasses project-based learning, but could go as far as learners designing their own syllabi within parameters set by the teacher, with their being able to request teacher intervention as and when they needed it. LED breaks down the power differential between teacher and learner not by turning learners into consumers, who regard teachers as being there to satisfy their whims, but by creating a dynamic partnership between teacher and learner.

The researchers conclude that LED is the next step in the evolution of conceptualisations of what formal education should be trying to achieve. It is, they suggest, an approach to education fit for the information age, the age of rapid change, the age when the success of an individual is determined by his ability to gather and process knowledge and to be creative. They employ the analogy of architecture; the architect, they point out, when given a commission to design a building, may, at one extreme, take complete control of the project from start to finish or, at the other extreme, allow herself to be the means through which the client realises her own vision. These are opposite ends of a continuum and there are of course intermediate states between the extremes. Perhaps the best way of applying LED in practice would be to view it as an evolving process, starting with a high level of teacher direction but with an end goal of near equality between teacher and learner.

The researchers report that learner feedback on LED was found to be very positive, indicating that learners enjoyed the control and independence it gave them. Compared to more traditional approaches, they tended to experience a higher degree of engagement and involvement with the learning process, not just intellectually but emotionally. The authors caution that some learners may find the chaos and confusion that can accompany LED too much and may, as a result, opt out. To avoid this, they suggest, the issue needs to be properly addressed in teacher/learner discussions.

Of course, it could be reasonably expected that learners in higher education would respond well to this sort of approach. After all, they start, presumably, with exceptionally high levels of motivation and self-confidence. They are also most likely drawn from sections of society whose members are accustomed to personal autonomy as opposed to those whose members are hampered by internalised oppression. My question would be: could it work in other educational contexts such as vocational programmes in further education, offender learning, or with young people still in compulsory education? I think that it ought to be possible to make it work in all of these contexts provided it is being implemented by teachers who truly believe in it and who are encouraged by managers who don't throw cold water over it. At the very least, teachers should have the freedom to experiment with different versions of it and to do their best to make it work. With something like this, it is much easier for the teacher carrying out the experiments when the whole organisation is interested in what she is doing and supportive of it, rather than in a situation where she is trying to work in an atmosphere of cynicism and tacit disapproval.

An important issue in the politics of learning is the rationing of opportunity, one aspect of which is the distinction between education and training. A better resourced post-compulsory vocational training sector is seen by many as the solution to a great many social and economic ills. There may be some truth in this, but we have to remember that, however much money the government throws at vocational training, its effectiveness depends entirely on the willingness of its intended beneficiaries to engage, not just in the sense of turning up and behaving themselves, but in the sense of being emotionally committed. If school leavers have been pushed down a vocational route because they have been labelled as 'not bright enough' for the academic one, we can hardly expect them to bring with them much in the way of real enthusiasm, especially if they never showed much enthusiasm for schooling in the first place. A post-compulsory vocational training system with a focus on hi-tech, prestige skills would be welcome, but to work it would require a school sector that produced sufficiently motivated entrance cohorts. If state schooling remains fundamentally unreformed and fails to engage with the issue of low motivation, no amount of money thrown at vocational training is likely to change the reality of the U.K. having a low-skill, low-wage economy for large numbers of workers.

The highest goal of education is for each learner to become everything he is capable of being, and there are two aspects to this. On the one hand, it is about an individual finding her purpose or vocation in life and developing the technical skills to go with this. On the other, it is about a transformation of the whole person that goes much deeper than the concept of 'skill'. The two things are inextricably linked, not either/or options. To send one set of learners down the first route and another set of learners down the second is utter folly.

It is interesting to note how, historically, the formal education system embodies social class stereotypes. In general, education for middle class people focused on the personal transformation aspect, while for working class people it was about preparing them for whatever jobs were available in their geographical area. This distinction still largely prevails, in my view, although it may not be quite as obvious as it once was. It is seen most clearly in the post-16 split, with working class people tending to either leave formal education or go down the vocational route, and middle class people going down the academic route. To put it simply, middle class people are ushered through the door marked 'Education', and working class people through the one marked 'Training'. Both groups lose out by being denied what the other gets. Let's unpick the essential differences between these two broad approaches to equipping learners for the future, starting with training:

Training is just as applicable to animals as it is to humans and aims to mould behaviour and instil correct values and attitudes. There is a 'correct' way to do everything and learners are expected to do things the correct way. Of course, everyone needs training if they are going to grow up to be able to function in civilised society, and it is a crucial feature of the formal educational experience. But the implication of providing training *instead of* education is the legitimisation of the belief that certain members of society should be prepared only to fit in, to know their place and be useful, that neither their own opinions as individuals nor their creative impulses matter very much.

Education, which puts these things at the very heart of the learning process, can be provided *alongside* training. It seeks to promote understanding and decision-making through reasoning from first principles, as opposed to blind obedience to rules and procedures. It sees each learner as unique and special, capable of reflection and self-awareness, able to find deeper meaning in what they do.

The idea that learners have of themselves as either 'not very bright' and needing to take the vocational training route, or 'bright' and needing to take the academic education route are aspects of identity that are largely constructed through classroom interactions between teachers and learners, and how this happens relates back to the earlier discussion of the effects of teacher expectations. Teachers need to become aware of the unwitting part they play in creating these harmful divisions and find ways of creating more of an 'equal but different' ethos. We might even reach the point eventually where we achieve parity of status between the two routes, thus allowing the vocational education sector to flourish like never before.

The distinction between pure training and training/education is at the centre of the debate between the advocates of phonics and the advocates of the use of stories in teaching children to read. Phonics requires the learner to associate numerous symbols with particular sounds. There is no room for self-expression here, and no place for a consideration of *meaning*, only for application and discipline. There is nothing wrong with using this approach if it works, but why not *also* make use of stories full of emotion and drama so as to ignite the child's enthusiasm? The same argument can be applied to the teaching of mathematics; committing multiplication tables to memory by rote is something that the child will find comes in very useful further in the future, but why not *also* allow her to be creative in maths lessons, and to find connections between maths and problems in the real world? Or, consider a child who wants to learn to play the violin. The tutor would not simply hand the violin and a bow to the child on the first lesson and tell her to have a go herself, imploring her to be creative; that would simply lead to frustration. But, if she isn't encouraged to use her emergent technical know-how in an expressive way soon enough, she will lose motivation. This is what I think is happening when a child becomes less and less engaged as he progresses through compulsory education – a failure to give sufficient attention to his need to find meaning in what he does because of the preoccupation with moulding him into what society wants him to be. Remember Billy Casper. On the other hand, when we neglect to give learners the technical underpinning they need to transform their lives, we are letting them down in a different way. Training and education are not mutually incompatible and to take the dogmatic position that all drilling and rote learning is wrong is itself a denial of opportunity.

My first job in education in 1994 was as a learning support assistant working with teenagers with severe learning difficulties. One of the things I was asked to do by the teacher in a literacy class was to get learners to trace out the shapes of letters of the alphabet on a piece of paper. What meaning did this have for a person who was never going to be literate in the sense of writing letters and reading books? Wouldn't it have been much more *meaningful* to have delivered literacy in a way that did have meaning for them because it connected with their experiences of everyday life, for example recognising the destination sign at the front of a bus, or the aisle signs in a supermarket?

The meaning of a learning experience is frequently contained in the process rather than the outcome. To take another example from my learning support assistant days, the learners I worked with got the chance to have pottery lessons as part of the curriculum. In these lessons, it mattered not one jot that the clay animals they made didn't look anything like the animals they were meant to be, or that the clay pots they made were lop-sided and leaky. It was the self-expression enmeshed in the creative process that mattered. Those learners were able to lose themselves in the moment and just 'be'. The pottery teacher was constantly under pressure from management to explain and rationalize the lessons on paper – to justify them in terms of learning goals such as 'being able to follow instructions', or 'being able to observe health and safety protocols', presumably with the ultimate aim of preparing them for menial employment in the future. To her eternal credit, though, she stood up for the idea that pottery can just be pottery.

The work of Ralph Tyler (1949) has had a huge influence on education in both the U.S. and U.K. from the 1940s to the present day. He argues that a successful learning experience requires the teacher to work from a set of precisely defined objectives. This teacher knows that learning has taken place when he can see that the objectives have been met. For example, an English lesson might start with an objective written as, *"By the end of the lesson, each learner will have listed ten synonyms for the word 'nice' and will have used each synonym in separate grammatically correct sentences."* This approach, which is philosophically rooted in the behaviourist paradigm discussed in Chapter 1, is very easy to learn and works wonderfully for teacher training micro-teach exercises. Unfortunately, in my experience, it fails to capture the essence of real learning in real classrooms because it has nothing to say about what makes learning meaningful to the learner. It is pure training rather than education/training.

One theorist who challenged Tyler's 'objectives model' was Lawrence Stenhouse (1975), who argued that learning didn't just progress in neat stages from A to B and then from B to C and so on. It was in reality far less predictable than that, with learners flitting about according to where their curiosity took them. Think of a butterfly fluttering from flower to flower in a garden. It follows that learning can never be precisely pre-determined in the way that Tyler's model implies. Stenhouse's 'process model' has the drawback of being much more difficult for the teacher to master than the objectives model, requiring him be an expert not just on his particular subject specialism but on the process of learning itself. Though it dispenses with the need for *pre-determined* learning objectives, it doesn't dispense with the notion of learning outcomes. It is just that, in the process model, outcomes emerge as a bi-product of a process that cannot be pre-determined. They can therefore only be identified in retrospect, as part of a reflective exercise.

For me, the value of the process model is in the freedom it gives learners to find their own meaning in the learning process. The centrality of 'meaning' in human experience was written about extensively by the existentialist psychotherapist Viktor Frankl (1946), who created a school of psychotherapy known as 'logotherapy' around it. For Frankl, the search for meaning was a basic human instinct. He proposed that human beings find meaning in their lives in three distinct ways:

- By creating or doing.

- By experiencing something or encountering someone.

- By the attitude we take when faced with difficult circumstances, i.e. responding constructively rather than destructively.

Is it possible to apply this theory within an educational setting? For Schreiber (2015), the answer to this question is 'Yes'. He argues that the emphasis within modern education systems of equipping learners with economically useful skills and knowledge, to the exclusion of personal growth, has resulted in a sense of emptiness which can find expression in aggression. He believes that the application of Frankl's ideas, perhaps with teachers undertaking formal training in them, would produce individuals capable of taking responsibility for themselves and others and of thinking for themselves with reference to their own core values.

Chapter 7

Reflection and the Art of Teaching

As we saw when we discussed creativity with regard to learners, creativity is, at base, the tendency of a person to want to work things out for themselves rather than follow rules. There is a connection between learner creativity and teacher creativity in so far as the teacher's creativity acts as a template for that of the learners. That is, by behaving in a creative manner, the teacher is indirectly communicating the message *"I want you to be creative"* to the unconscious minds of the learners.

No-one is completely uncreative, but I think that it is reasonable to speak in terms of some people being very creative and others being only minimally creative. I am not suggesting that creativity is genetically inherited, just that, for whatever reason, some people develop their creative potential while others don't. It is probably best to think of creativity not as a single personality trait but as a combination of different ones, including openness (a willingness contemplate new ideas) and intuitiveness (a tendency to be in touch with one's unconscious mind).

I was, for a time, heavily involved in my local amateur drama group. What I enjoyed about acting was the opportunity it presented for creativity; an actor, after all, needs to get inside the mind of the character he's playing and understand the world from that character's point of view, something that takes a leap of imagination. I learned, however, that not all amateur actors are interested in creativity. In fact, some of them really couldn't care less about it. A director could tell them exactly what to say and how to say it and dictate their every move because, for them, it is not about creativity but *performance*; they want to feel a connection to the audience and get a kick out of the appreciation coming back to them. I think that there is a similar issue in teaching. The problem here is that, if you have a profession where the vast majority of practitioners are happy to be told what to do and what to think as long as they get the chance to perform, you have a situation where any change is driven from the top down rather than the bottom up and the teacher becomes a mere follower of orders, obediently implementing policies decreed from on high. Teachers need to work on their creativity like athletes need to work on their physical fitness.

When we talk about the need for teachers to be creative, it is often in the belief that such creativity takes place exclusively in the planning and preparation of lessons, but it is equally important for teachers to be creative in the moment, to change and adapt in the act of delivering a lesson. This type of creativity is analogous to acting improvisationally as opposed to following a script. To simply plough on with a planned lesson regardless of what is happening in the moment is a recipe for disaster and humiliation.

The teacher must manage the lesson with regard not just for each learner as an individual but for the group as a learning organism in its own right. It is the regular alternation between phases of teacher as leader of a whole-group experience and phases of teacher as facilitator of numerous individual learning experiences that gives the lesson its sense of rhythm. Rather like the conductor of an orchestra, the teacher needs to have a feel for the beat of the lesson and an intuitive grasp of when the switches in focus need to happen.

It doesn't take much creativity to stand in front of a group of learners and tell them things, nor for that matter to get them all doing individual activities. In preference to either of these approaches, the creative teacher will do his utmost to get learners to learn from each other and will strive to become skilled at working out how to achieve this for any given group. In theory, it ought to be possible for learners to pool their various pieces of prior learning and combine them to create new understandings. The teacher ought to be able to throw a problem into the group as if it were a hand grenade and let the learners work together to solve it. Unfortunately, it is not quite that simple in practice. Instead of collaborating, the learners may respond instead by competing against each other, splintering into friendship cliques, behaving as if they were on a break, choosing a leader to follow from amongst themselves, complaining about the lack of guidance, or sabotaging the lesson in a whole host of other ways. When faced with these sorts of behaviours, a mediocre teacher would abandon the idea of using group-based learning altogether and resort either to a more didactic approach or to giving learners individual activities. The creative teacher, on the other hand, will refuse to admit defeat and will try to find a solution to the problem. One source of inspiration she might turn to is the discipline of group dynamics, and my own favourite theorist in this field is Wilfred Bion (1961).

For Bion, unconscious forces are always at play in social behaviour and these forces tend to get in the way of groups achieving what they were set up to achieve. He postulates that, in any given situation in which people came together in groups to achieve goals, there exist in reality two groups in one, almost as if the group, like an individual person, had its own mind which was divided into conscious and unconscious parts. The first of the two groups is the 'work group', goal-focused and rational. The second is the 'basic assumption group', whose purpose is to reduce anxiety. If the basic assumption group holds sway, three strategies can be employed to deal with anxiety. The first is 'dependency', where the group selects and follows a strong leader. The second is 'fight or flight' where the group engages in either aggressive or avoidant behaviour patterns. The third is 'pairing', where the group splinters into sub-groups, each comprised of two or three closely bonded individuals who are unable to engage properly with the group task because they are too wrapped up in each other. The two groups (work and basic assumption) are in a constant state of interplay and tension.

For the teacher who wants to use Bion's theories in promoting group-based learning, the central task is to make sure that the work group is not constantly thwarted by the basic assumption group. Trying to confront the disruptive behaviour directly will tend to intensify the very anxiety that is at the root of the behaviour so such a tactic will be counterproductive. In my own experience, more success is to be had using a longer term strategy. That is, I start off by presenting myself as being in command, as being knowledgeable and authoritative and in so doing feed the group's need for a paternalistic leader. Then, by degrees, I transfer responsibility over to the group, to the point where I eventually become little more than a supplier of raw materials in the form of problems to solve.

Another approach is to use the pairing tendency in an advantageous way. One initially allows the group to form and work in pairs or trios. As anxiety falls, these sub-groups will hopefully become more relaxed about interacting not just amongst themselves but with other sub-groups and this leads quite naturally to the entire group working as one. This approach is sometimes called 'snowballing'. Image a snowball getting bigger and bigger as it rolls along the snow-covered ground; the expanding snowball symbolises the increasing creative power of the whole group as it swallows up the smaller ones.

I find Bion's ideas fascinating, but I have no desire to force them down the throats of readers. What I would say is that a teacher who aspires to be creative needs to take an interest in theory and to adopt those theories which, to him, make sense and concord with his underlying philosophy, as well standing the test practical application. This selection of preferred theories and models forms the basis of his unique personal style which he has every right to practise without interference from those who may disapprove. It sometimes seems that there is a view amongst those in authority that there is one correct way to teach and that the evaluation of teachers should be something like the driving test, in which the person being evaluated is deemed to have failed if he deviates from the approved method. I think that these warriors for 'the one true faith' have inflicted, and continue to inflict, enormous damage on the quality of education experienced by learners and on the morale of teachers.

I love planning lessons, but hate being told *how* to plan them. There are as many different ways of planning lessons as there are teachers and a teacher should be encouraged to develop a personal planning style to complement and support her personal teaching style. She should be expected to imbue her work with her own individual uniqueness, to view teaching as a form of self-expression. The best thing a teacher can do when presented by her employer with a standardised lesson plan template is to tear it up and write one in her own style on a blank piece of paper. If this is politically impossible in her workplace culture, she could always do what I used to do and write two lesson plans, the real one that I actually used and the one using the official paperwork.

I have always taken it absolutely for granted and as a self-evident truth that teaching is a creative profession and, as such, is comparable to other creative professions such as musicianship, painting or acting. Creativity is, to a large extent, inherently selfish because it entails pursuing one's own truth rather than helping the person in authority to pursue there's, hence the need to be a little anti-authoritarian sometimes. We must of course contend with political reality and the creative professional must, to some degree at least, give the people paying his wages what they want. But, if he did this to the total exclusion of personal self-expression, he would become stale and cynical and his work would inevitably be of mediocre quality. The creative professional needs to stay in touch with his individuality and with his own values and to have the confidence to express these through his work.

There are, then, two sides to teaching and teachers need to be proficient in both of them. The first side is about using the left halves of their brains and involves having clearly defined learning outcomes and well-structured lessons. The second, more creative, side is about using the right half of the brain and involves being able to enthuse learners and convey passion – to *dramatize* the learning experience – spontaneously in the midst of a lesson.

The classroom is a theatre and the teacher needs the skills of an actor, but this is not acting as in pretending to be something he is not. On the contrary, it is about projecting an *authentic* version of himself and, to achieve this, he needs to look *inwards* and use memory and imagination to construct a believable stage persona. If he did try to 'fake it', the learners would see through him and his relationship with them would never get off the ground. The quality of *charisma,* I think, has something to do with there being such a close match between a person's true self and the persona he is projecting that he feels a sense of invincibility and comes across as having absolute confidence when he's performing to an audience.

For a teacher to try to be something he is not is, then, a serious error. However, we should also be aware that, where it comes to personality types, there is a school of thought that says that we all have the ability to become the opposite of our normal preference (Jung, 1923). A teacher who, like myself, is naturally introverted, for example, may find it advantageous sometimes to use his imagination to find his inner extravert.

At the risk of stating the obvious, teaching creatively *isn't* like stacking skelves at a supermarket; to be able to teach, a person needs to be in a good place psychologically. A creative person moves into a good place psychologically when she feels accepted for who she and when she is given the space to be herself. She has a right to *insist* on being treated this way and to cry foul when these conditions are not met.

If a teacher feels good enough about herself to be able to relax and be spontaneous when she's with a group of learners, amazing things can happen. Csikszentmihalyi (1990) describes a phenomenon he terms 'flow' – the mental state of being so totally engrossed in an activity that one loses all sense of time. When we are in flow, we feel happy, we feel in control, we are being spontaneously and effortlessly creative. A teacher has struck gold when both she and her learners achieve this state. The concept of flow utterly contradicts the view that says, *"If I want to be a good teacher, I need to selflessly deny my own happiness and do my duty, as dull and unpleasant as it may be"*, and replaces this joyless stoicism with an attitude of, *"If it feels good, it probably is good"*.

There are many words and phrases to describe flow: improvising, behaving intuitively, responding to gut feelings, being 'in the zone', to name but a few. A teacher in flow is like a surfer somehow managing to keep his balance and stay on his feet whilst being buffeted by powerful waves coming at him from all directions and to which he only has a split second to react. A teacher in the classroom doesn't have to contend with waves but will certainly be buffeted by questions, comments and challenges coming at her thick and fast and will need to react instantly to each one, drawing constantly on memories stored in her bank of experiences.

Another good parallel is that of the be-bop style of jazz which emerged in the 1950s as an attempt to reclaim the art form from descent into commercialisation and inauthenticity. In be-bop, only the basic chord structure of a piece of music is retained whilst different soloists spontaneously improvise melodies based on their feel for the beat. This way of working is tremendously liberating and must have been an inspiration for both abstract expressionist painters and the 'beat generation' of writers. It should be an inspiration also for teachers.

In the received wisdom about teaching, of course, there is a bias in favour of forward planning and against spontaneity, reflective of a general suspicion of the irrational in western culture, but a teacher cannot plan to achieve flow. In fact, over-planning works against creativity because it means that the teacher comes into the classroom exhausted from over-work, resentful over loss of recreation time and anxious over whether the learners will co-operate with the plan. Those who obsess over planning and preparation and its corresponding mountains of paperwork overestimate the value of pre-meditation and underestimate the value being 'in the moment'. One does not have to suffer from obsessive compulsive personality disorder to be a great teacher; If a teacher can somehow learn to let go and just be himself in the classroom, there is a fighting chance that his unconscious will take over and deliver the goods. If not, the lesson plan is there as a safety net. The joy of teaching is not in planning and being in control but in trusting in the randomness of the learning process. Rather than writing down her lesson plans in minute detail, perhaps a better use of a teacher's non-contact time would be to write down, or express in some other way, her personal philosophy and to share it with her learners and colleagues.

At the beginning of my teaching career, I was an enthusiastic planner. This was something of an article of faith with me. I had, after all, had the dogma of detailed planning and preparation hammered into me in teacher training, and to go into a lesson without a detailed plan would have been to me as unthinkable as going in naked. Later, I grew to understand the limitations of too much thinking ahead and began to work more improvisationally. Now, any written plan I use will consist of a short list of key things I need to remember to do and say. For the most part, I place my trust in the creative potential of my unconscious which I have fed and nurtured over many years.

What do I mean by feeding and nurturing the creative potential of my unconscious? Well, much of this is to do with the unconscious accumulation of classroom experiences, but I also believe that the part of my brain that gives me the ability to teach effectively is never really switched off. When I go off duty, I may stop giving my conscious attention to my teaching job, but my teacher brain is still whirring away in the background, mulling over past experiences, coming up with ideas for future lessons. Now, if I go out of my way to stimulate my teacher brain by engaging in cultural activities – reading, watching films, visiting art galleries and by generally observing the world around me – then I am feeding and nurturing it and, almost uncannily, it will throw up ideas for me in the heat of the lesson when I need it.

This feeding and nurturing thing is what I do instead of obsessively over-the-top planning and preparation. Another word for it is *reflection*. Some teachers, particularly extraverted ones, view this as a process of being consciously self-critical and therefore dislike it, but I think that this is to misunderstand what it is all about. For me, reflection entails, in the first instance, letting go of the conscious effort to think about something specific and allowing my thoughts to wander freely. I find that, when I do this, new ideas pop into my consciousness as if from nowhere. If one of these ideas strikes me as particularly interesting and relevant to my work as a teacher, I will conduct a 'thought experiment' with it. That is, I will start playing around with it, bending it and stretching it, exploring its possibilities to exhaustion. A variation on this is that the thought that pops into my head is a memory of something that happened to me, something that a learner or a colleague had said perhaps, or it could be something I read or a film I'd watched. I will replay this memory over and over again in my head, coming up with different interpretations of what I had learnt from what had happened.

I am convinced that this process is central to all learning beyond simple behavioural conditioning, and to all of what we call creativity. For this reason, all teachers need not just to be able to do it themselves but to be able to teach *learners* to do it too. When you think about it, all effective teaching is the encouragement of reflection on the part of learners – of getting them to think for themselves. This is why good teachers prefer to ask questions than give answers and why they are not afraid of silence. If a learner is genuinely struggling to muster enough imagination to reflect independently, a teacher can help by hinting and prompting, just to get the ball rolling, but this should be done sparingly.

Reflection can be thought of as a means of escape from a state of confusion. In Greek mythology, when Theseus was about to enter the Labyrinth to hunt down the fearsome Minotaur, his lover Ariadne gave him a ball of thread which he unravelled behind him as he went deeper and deeper into the network of tunnels. This trail of thread was his escape route. If the Labyrinth symbolises a state of confusion, Ariadne's thread symbolises reflection; without it, we would simply be swallowed up by the darkness and remain forever prisoners of it.

Returning to the teacher's own habit of reflection, it has in my own case always been a very private activity. The reason for this is that I tend to feel that to share my thought processes with colleagues is tantamount to inviting them to do the reflection for me and I would be surrendering my independence. But, then again, I am an introvert and tend to behave in an introverted way. Extraverted teachers may find that they prefer to reflect in a pair or as part of a group. It is not the method of reflection that matters but the insights and creative ideas it throws up.

Claxton (1997) calls reflection 'tortoise-minded' thinking. The other kind of thinking, thinking in pursuit of specific goals, he calls 'hare-brained'. The image of the slow-moving tortoise is perfect for conveying the fact that becoming better at reflection is about learning to slow down. Educational institutions are typically very busy places where teachers are constantly running around, frantically trying to get things done. This is not conducive to creativity! Teachers need to find time for leisure. They need to find time during the day to chat casually with colleagues. They need proper lunch breaks and to leave work on time every day. One of the problems with the present state of the teaching profession in the U.K. is that a virtue has been made out of putting in long hours, not on being creative but on the drudgery of detailed record-keeping. It is not a question so much of teachers doing too much work per se – no-one begrudges spending time doing something they find joy in – but of their doing too much of the wrong sort of work. I often have to tell my driving pupils to slow down. By this, I don't always mean *"Slow the car down"*; sometimes I mean *"Slow your brain down and relax"*. Being hare-brained has its uses, but there are times when the tortoise mind is needed, either to get us out of the trouble that moving too quickly has gotten us into, or to take us to places which our hare-brains don't have access.

It is a wonderful thing to be able to teach brilliant, inspiring lessons when conditions are in our favour, but the reality of teaching is that sometimes the learners are just not quite on our wavelength. The ideal psychological state to be in in the classroom, remember, is one of *flow*. This is either something that teacher and learners both have simultaneously or it doesn't exist at all. When we lose this and the lesson descends into mediocrity, one way of lifting it is for the teacher to engage with the learners, in a relaxed, leisurely kind of way, about what concerns *them*, whatever that may be, as opposed to hoping that they will start to engage with her agenda if she just stubbornly keeps pushing it. By using this more empathic approach, she is getting learners to let go of tension and creating the conditions under which flow can naturally re-emerge. She is playing the long game, using her tortoise mind.

I want to consider now Stephen Brookfield's (1998) concept of 'critically reflective practice'. To quote him directly:

"Critically reflective practice is a process of inquiry involving practitioners in trying to discover, and research, the assumptions that frame how they work. Critically reflective practitioners constantly research these assumptions by seeing practice through four complementary lenses: the lens of their own autobiographies as learners of reflective practice, the lens of learners' eyes, the lens of colleagues' perceptions, and the lens of theoretical, philosophical, and research literature. Reviewing practice through these lenses makes us more aware of those submerged and unacknowledged power dynamics that infuse all practice settings. It also

helps us detect hegemonic assumptions—assumptions that we think are in our own best interests but that actually work against us in the long term."

The implication of what Brookfield proposes is that the scope of a teacher's reflections should not be limited to what happens in the classroom but should be widened to encompass her experiences of the wider power dynamics of the institution within which she works. If we can find a way to detach ourselves from the institution's culture and view it with the eyes of outsiders, we will inevitably find ourselves rejecting many of its values and implicit assumtions. This will put us on a trajectory which leads to our becoming increasingly dissatisfied with simply performing the technical aspects of our jobs well, or with pleasing those who are judging us. Instead, we will start to be driven much more by our own independent values and assumptions and by our personal philosophies. The emergence of this yearning, in the mind of the teacher, to go his own way equates, I think, to what Maslow (1970) calls *the drive to self-actualisation*.

I would argue, however, that true self-actualisation has not taken place until the teacher begins to actively rail against the institutional culture that is holding her back from doing her job the way she wants to do it. This could lead to her becoming engaged in workplace politics, in advocating change, in trying to create a counterculture which pushes back against prevailing orthodoxies.

In a democracy, it is not just the right but the *duty* of people to question authority, but going alongside this duty is the obligation to question authority with grace and humour, and without resorting to undignified personal attacks. Those in authority ought, in turn, to accept being questioned in the same spirit. Our educational institutions should be micro-democracies in the sense that the are marked, culturally, by a spirit of civilised debate in which no-one need fear saying what they think and people are listened to and taken seriously when they say what they think. If this is not the prevailing spirit, then it is up to the staff members to make it so.

A teacher who reflects systematically with unflinching honesty can achieve extraordinary levels of self-insight. It is fascinating for me to look back over my old reflective journal writings. There is a definite sense there of making a philosophical journey. At the very beginning, there is a certain naivety, perhaps summed up by the phrase, *"If I'm nice to them they'll like me."* This quickly melts away to be replaced by an angry vengefulness, a feeling that the learners are a bunch of wild animals with whom it is impossible to reason. There seems then to be a process by which I slowly and painfully work my way through this crisis to become tactically astute and adept at manipulating my way through lessons. Later still, my thinking develops in an altogether more radical direction and I start to critique the system itself, seeing both learners and teachers as victims of it. All this happened over the first three or four years of my keeping the journal. After that, my underlying philosophy settled and was relatively stable, needing merely to be refined and occasionally reinforced. At the same time, however, there is growing evidence of a certain attitude of animosity towards those in authority, particularly where I perceived that they were clinging on to out-moded attitudes. The journal often has the feel of being written not by someone thinking strategically and looking for ways to out-think his opponents, but of someone looking for a safe way to vent his frustrations and feelings of animosity towards the powerful. There are strong hints of status anxiety and of being internally conflicted over whether to be a team player or to express my individuality. I did not really discuss the content of my journal with work colleagues or managers but, looking back now, I wonder if I was revealing some of it unconsciously in the way I came across. I think the truth of the matter is that my issues with dealing with people in authority go back much further than when I started my teaching career; I think they go all the way back to my first experiences in school and I think that is why I tend to identify with learners with the same issues.

Reflection does not come easily or naturally to everyone, but I think that it is a skill that can be mastered by anyone if they apply themselves to it. A simple way to start is to get into the habit, at the end of every day, of thinking back over the day's events and making two lists: 'things that went well', and 'things that went badly'. Once you had established this habit, you could then start sub-dividing and refining the lists, e.g. 'things that went badly because I was in the wrong', and 'things that went badly because of circumstances beyond my control'. Of course, getting into the habit of doing this will not change your basic personality type, nor should you wish it to, but it will give a powerful extra dimension to your professional practice.

Earlier, I suggested that a naturally introverted teacher might find it useful occasionally to express his inner extravert. The notion that part of a teacher's role is to spend some time in solitary reflection, however, implies that a naturally extraverted teacher might need sometimes to find his *inner introvert*. It might seem odd to suggest that the disposition towards introversion might be of value in a profession as dependent on communication skills as teaching, but this is a prejudice based on a common misconception. Susan Cain (op. cit.), herself an introvert, argues that, in western culture, there is a tendency in the workplace to over-value the contributions of extraverts, for example their tendency to confidently insist that their ideas are the best, and to under-value those of introverts, for example their willingness to listen to others, as well as to their own inner voices. In teaching, extraverts undeniably bring an ability to energise the learning experience and command the attention of learners. They also excel at collaborating with colleagues. On the other hand, introverts find it easier to stand back and let the learners be the stars of the show and to listen to them. They are also better than extraverts at dissociating themselves from the workplace 'groupthink' – the tendency for people who spend a lot of time together to develop a mindset in which the desire for consensus overrides the need to challenge and question assumptions (Janis, 1972). Furthermore, the introvert's natural tendency towards introspection and contemplation tends to makes him good at reflection and this skill, as we have seen, is essential in teaching.

A variation on solitary reflection which might appeal to teachers who feel at their most creative in the company of others is to develop peer-mentoring groups of perhaps three or four members. It would be a simple thing to set this up in a workplace, or using a social media platform, provided there were sufficient numbers of people able to see the benefit and enthusiastic about getting involved. These groups could be developed either with or without the knowledge and consent of management. Within their confines, teachers would feel free to be honest about what they really thought and they could bounce thoughts off one another and help each other to develop their ideas. It is possible that these groups could develop in such a way that they started to direct their energies outwards and become more political, like mini-pressure groups for change within the organisation. Care would need to be taken, however, to ensure that the group members were truly equal to one another, that they didn't start to develop subtle pecking orders that were microcosms of the organisational hierarchy.

Developing a personal philosophy is crucial for people at the beginning of their teaching careers, but just a word now about experienced teachers, for whom I hope this book also has some resonance. As a teacher progresses through his career, he acquires layer upon layer of behaviours, assumptions and attitudes which he assimilates into his professional persona. Some of this comes from training, some from dictats handed down from on high, but most of it comes from workplace culture (doing what everyone else does). There eventually comes a point, I think, when a person is carrying so much of this baggage that he starts to become creatively stale. At this point, he needs to get back in touch with who he truly is, the person he was when he first went in to teaching. The path to improvement for such a teacher is no longer to add more and more layers of clutter, but to strip most of it off, screw it up into a ball and throw it away. Beyond a certain point, the key to becoming a better teacher subtraction rather than addition.

Chapter 8

The Teacher's Use of self

When a teacher enters into an employment contract, he is agreeing to provide his skills, expertise and professional judgment. He is not selling his soul. He is neither forgoing his right, nor relinquishing his duty, to think for himself and to adhere to his own values and convictions. A reflective practitioner is, in essence, one who understands this and does whatever she can to make it a reality in practice. What does this take? To borrow some words from Shakespeare's *Twelfth Night*:

 "Some are born great, some achieve greatness and some have greatness thrust upon 'em."

In the play, Shakespeare uses the word 'greatness' in the sense of outward greatness, what we today might call authority or status. But I think we can, for our purposes, invert this notion of so that it means instead an inner greatness, that is an independence of spirit coupled with high levels of self-awareness and personal integrity. This is what marks out reflective practitioners and leaders of countercultures.

Being born great might allude to a person's natural disposition – possession of a blend of personal characteristics which give a person a head start in their journey towards becoming a workplace leader. Such characteristics might include both conventional and emotional intelligence, as well as patience, stamina and perseverance.

Then there are the ways in which teachers can achieve greatness, that is acquire leadership qualities, by viewing their sense of who they are not as a set of givens but as a work in progress. If we think back to Gazzaniga's work on split-brain patients (see Chapter 4), we see that the mind is capable of hosting two distinct 'selves', one in each cerebral hemisphere. But, if the mind can host two selves, why not several, each with its own distinct identity and function? Bachkirova (2011) suggests that the human mind can be thought of as a network of 'mini-selves', each one a self-contained system with its own part to play in meeting the individual's needs. It seems plausible to me that one of these mini-selves might serve the function of taking information from all of the others and weaving the strands together to tell stories and create meanings.

These mini-selves, it is important to realise, are not like the systems in a machine, such as an automobile, where they are interlinked in very precise ways to form a coherent whole, but independent entities. My own take on the implication of this is that the idea that a person has one single, enduring, immutable Self is an illusion; it is a fiction, a story a person tells himself about himself. This insight allows us to talk in a terms of a person's 'self-concept', their own fictional narrative about who they are with which they can experiment creatively.

Viewing Self in this way allows for the possibility that a person can have more than one version of who they are and switch between them depending on circumstance. An individual may also make a distinction between versions of herself that are internal and subjective, i.e. about how she feels inside, and versions that she presents to others, and she may wish to reflect on how much incompatibility between the two she is prepared to tolerate. Too great an incongruence between private and public selves can, over a course of time, cause feelings of unease and an increasing sense of alienation from what thinks of as one's true Self.

Some people create shadow selves which are hidden from consciousness and only become manifest through phenomena such as somnambulism, hypnosis or ventriloquism. For cinematic portrayals of ventriloquists who express such alter egos through their dolls, see *Magic* (1978, dir. Richard Attenborough, starring Anthony Hopkins as the ventriloquist), and *Dead of Night* (1945, dir. Alberto Cavalcanti, starring Michael Redgrave as the ventriloquist). The most famous literary explorations of alter ego are, however, Robert Louis Stephenson's *The Strange Case of Dr. Jeckyll and Mr. Hyde* (1886) and Oscar Wilde's *The Picture of Dorian Gray* (1890). Often, the alter ego is a nastier version of the conscious self, a repository for the desires and impulses the conscious self does not wish to acknowledge.

Of course, viewing the Self as fiction allows us to think in terms of being able to tear apart any existing self-concept and rebuild it from its fragments and I think that this is what is happening when people undergo, and then recover from, bouts of mental illness. This is a very sudden and dramatic transformation of Self, but it can also be useful to think of the Self as something that develops more gradually over time through a process of deep reflection, building on top of what is already there rather than destroying it and starting again. This requires hard work, patience and persistence, but the rewards are more than worth it.

Bachkirova argues that the work of developing the Self begins with *perception* – noticing more of what is going on in the environment, and listening more. The individual then needs to reflect on the ways in which perceptions can be inaccurate reflections of reality:

- Do unconscious desires distort my perceptions?

- How much am I prone to self-deception?

- How much of what I think I know is cultural conditioning?

- Do I adopt strategies to avoid thinking about things I finds emotionally traumatic?

As we saw in the last chapter, one possible trajectory a teacher's self-development can follow is that of a gradual movement away from his seeing himself as someone who needs to gain acceptance by pleasing those in authority, towards his seeing himself as someone with the confidence to reject values foisted upon him and act in accordance with his own.

The third way of gaining inner greatness and to become a workplace leader is to have it thrust upon you. It is entirely possible that any given teacher might, at some point in her career, experience some sort or trauma or major disappointment which precipitates a psychological crisis of some sort. The way out of this is for her to begin a process of looking deep within herself and confronting her inner demons (think of Theseus in the Labyrinth). Through this process, she comes to gradually re-evaluate her fundamental values and assumptions and starts to reformulate her professional goals. Working with someone else on this, someone she could confide in and trust to respond empathically, might prove less daunting than trying to go it alone.

Carl-Gustav Jung (op. cit.) places *individuation* – his term for the process by which a human being becomes everything he is capable of being – at the centre of his method of psychotherapy. For him, this means integrating the conscious part of the psyche with the unconscious elements, something not to be taken lightly as it involves struggle and suffering. The unconscious elements to which he refers include our individual 'shadow' – our deepest fears and anxieties, so psychologically threatening to us that we push them out of consciousness. But Jung also wrote about what he termed *the collective unconscious*, a wealth of unconscious symbols or *archetypes* shared by the whole of mankind and through which we frame our understanding of ourselves and of our relationships. We encounter such archetypes in our dreams, as well as in art and culture, and when we are being creative. The *Shadow* (see above) is itself an archetype, but other examples include the *Self*, i.e. the sum total of all the elements that make up our psyche when they have been integrated into a whole, and the *Persona*, the version of ourselves which we present to the world.

Two key archetypes are the *Anima,* the hidden feminine side of the male personality and the *Animus,* the hidden masculine side of the female personality. An individual who is dominated by the masculine side of his personality and has been unable or unwilling to incorporate his anima into his conscious identity is in danger of succumbing to what we might term 'toxic masculinity', characterised by an excess of aggression, competitiveness and authoritarianism. On the other hand, we could talk of 'toxic femininity' – an excess of passivity, submission and conflict avoidance, where a person dominated by her female side has not integrated her animus. It should be noted that these issues are not necessarily related to the person's biological sex or gender identity. It is quite possible, for example, for a person who identifies as a woman to exhibit toxic masculinity, just as it is possible for a person who identifies as a man to exhibit toxic femininity. A fully individuated person will have full access to both anima and animus and will thus be much more flexible in her ability to respond appropriately to all situations and challenges.

We need also to realise that individuation is not the same as striving for perfection. On the contrary, it aims to reconcile us with our imperfections (the shadow archetype) and to help us to bring them into consciousness. The more we do this, the less a cause for anxiety our imperfections become and the less we need to conceal them. The process is in essence one of developing an ability to quietly stand apart from ourselves and observe our own mental processes as objectively as possible, watching our own opinions form and working out which are genuine insights and which are manifestations of prejudices or misunderstandings. It is, in other words, a form of deep reflection.

There are those who believe that individuation requires a person to undergo one-to-one psychotherapy involving intense self-revelation and dream analysis, and that the eventual outcome is that they withdraw from society and becomes some sort of mystic. Those things are there for those who want them, but I believe that individuation simply means having the courage to go towards challenges rather than running away from them, whether those challenges are in the outside world or within our own minds.

Whether internal or external in origin, these challenges are the sort for which there is no ready-made solution, leaving us with no choice but to ask fundamental questions about who we really are and what we really believe, and allow ourselves to be utterly transformed. What this means in terms of changes in how we behave in the world and relate to others will vary from person to person. For some, it could mean taking on a new role within their employing organisation, while for others it could mean leaving the organisation and doing something completely different with their lives. For others still it could mean changing the way they see their job and shifting from an attitude of passive acceptance to one of actively striving to promote their personal philosophy in the workplace. Whatever course of action the person takes, though, should be a reflection of who they feel they really are and what they feel they are meant to be doing, rather than an adherence to some conventional notion of what success means.

I am fond of the legend in which the Blues artist Robert Johnson meets the Devil at the crossroads. Johnson sells his soul to the Devil in return for creative genius. I believe that the Devil in this story is not the personification of evil but of the *unconscious*. Selling your soul to the Devil means, at a metaphorical level, allowing yourself to be led by your unconscious and thus becoming your authentic self.

For existentialist thinkers such as Sartre (1943), the central fact of human existence is *choice*. The other side of the Robert Johnson legend is that he *chose* to do his deal with the Devil. In doing so, he acknowledged that he had the choice. He could have denied that he had the choice. He could have taken the attitude that his fate was pre-determined and that he just needed to learn to live with whatever circumstance threw at him. But he had the courage to make the choice and live with the consequences and that, in my view, is what makes him a hero. In the course of his career, a teacher will sooner or later come to a moment of choice, a crossroads if you will, and he will either walk away from that choice through fear of responsibility, and live with the knowledge of his own cowardice, or face up to it and live with the consequences of whatever decision he made.

We cannot choose the political reality of the situation we find ourselves in but we can certainly choose our response to it. People often talk of 'workplace stress'. I don't believe in stress. Stress is the name people give to the feeling they get when they refuse to acknowledge the fact that they always have a choice and instead allow themselves to be defined by other people's expectations of them, thereby making themselves terrified of failing to meet those expectations. Instead, I believe in the spirit of *The Blues*, a positive response to adversity that is defiantly individualistic – a philosophy of choosing to rise above, of saying, *"Throw whatever you like at me. It won't make any difference because there's something inside me that's too strong to succumb to your intimidation"*. There is a sense in there of *redemption* – of finding one's true character at one's lowest moments – connected to the complete loss of ego and the letting go of all forms of self-deception. From here, a person can build a new self-concept with foundations of granite.

Whatever your definition of success, there has to be more to it than being good at pleasing others. It is by adopting the mentality that our individual selves don't matter that we open ourselves up to being manipulated and dominated by those whom we mistakenly believe have the right to judge us. Our notion of what it means to be successful needs to encompass not just our ability to please others, but the extent to which we feel we are being true to our own values. Realising this fact smashes the chains of internalised oppression and gives us the confidence to express our individuality. It allows us to look authority in the eye and speak truth to power. Getting to this point is itself a victory.

In his classic book *The Divided Self* (1960), the radical psychiatrist RD Laing wrote about the mental health dangers for a person of being forced into playing a role for the sake of conforming to what other people want him to be, and of losing contact with his authentic self in the process. The tension between these two versions of a person's self is behind what Laing termed 'ontological insecurity', a fear of losing one's real self altogether. In performing unreal versions of ourselves day-in-day-out, we slowly lose our sense of conviction in the idea that there is, somewhere within us, a real person who exists independently from the performances, and whom we can find if we just peel away all the layers of fakery. Instead, we feel as if we are simply robots, controlled by others for the benefit of others.

The question is, *how* do we hold on to a sense of ourselves as real people, separate from others' expectations? The answer, I believe, is that we need, as workplace communities, to create space and time where we can celebrate each other's 'realness'. I am talking here about the quality of *acceptance*. We accept someone when we allow them to hold views that are different from our own without making them feel bad about holding those views. We accept someone when we allow them to do things in a way that is different to the way we would do them without passing judgment. This quality of acceptance either applies universally or not at all.

It needs to be part of the culture of the workplace, a culture where the right to an individual identity is given the highest priority.

Chapter 9

Changing the System from Within

On March 8th 2021, the children of England returned to school after a long absence due to the coronavirus pandemic. In anticipation of this event, the teacher and former journalist Lucy Kellaway wrote a piece entitled *'What is the Point of Schools?'* for the weekend edition of the *Financial Times*, published two days in advance of the great return. In her piece, Kellaway makes a number of statements I would wholeheartedly agree with, bemoaning the obsession with filling students with facts so that they can pass exams, and writing of her frustration with the infliction by the schooling system of a boring, uninspiring curriculum on children. But then she goes and spoils it by stating, *"I will do this because it is my job."* What a cop-out! The notion that we have no choice but to do the same thing day after day without feeling that we are really achieving anything is not only absurd and utterly depressing, but just plain wrong.

Teachers have a duty to try to change the world of formal education for the better, and they should see this as part of their contract with society. With sufficient determination, much can be achieved, but before we can change anything, we need to understand what it is we're trying to change and how we got to this position in the first place.

State education as we know it in the U.K. began with the Forster Act of 1870, which made schooling free and compulsory for children between the ages of five and twelve. Why would the state provide education for those who would otherwise be unable to afford it? And why would they believe that it needed to be made compulsory? I would suggest that one reason for its introduction was to improve economic productivity; Britain needed to compete with other industrial nations if it wanted to keep its 'workshop of the world' status. Another reason might have been the extension of the voting franchise to working class people in 1867; the masses needed to be educated to vote 'properly', i.e. not for extremist movements. A third reason might have been the need to attend to what might be termed the 'moral health of the nation' – promoting the work ethic and the doctrine of self-help. Overarching all these considerations, however, was the inescapable truth that the urban working classes needed to *controlled,* and the new schools, like the prisons and workhouses already in existence, were designed to do just that. This explains the perceived need to make formal education compulsory and to set up a system to enforce compliance. The historical association between formal education and social control may help to explain why, to this day, children from working class backgrounds don't always engage well with schooling.

In 1944, the Butler Act at last introduced an element of aspiration towards facilitating social mobility, reflecting the mood of the time, but the catch was that this opportunity was limited to a select few who passed the eleven-plus and got to go to grammar school. The perceived brutality of the selective system became a cause for concern on the political left and, in the 1960s, the grammar school/secondary modern apartheid system began to be phased out in much of the country, much to the dismay of social conservatives. The Black Papers, a series of articles published in the journal *Critical Quarterly* from the late 1960s to the early 1970s (see Cox and Dyson, 1971), were essentially attacks on what their authors saw as the excesses of 'progressive education', by which they meant the tendency to prioritise the push for social equality over academic standards.

The desire to curb the malign influence of progressivism was not solely confined to the political right, however. In 1976, Labour Prime Minister James Callaghan made a speech at Ruskin College in which he expressed concern over the over-use of what he termed 'informal methods of teaching' and argued that schools should do more to give pupils the skills they needed for jobs in industry. Callaghan was at heart a consensus politician who wanted to take the teaching unions with him in whatever reforms he was thinking of introducing. In fact, he never got the chance to introduce them as he was voted out of office in 1979. Margaret Thatcher, his Conservative successor, by contrast, could never be accused of shying away from confrontations with unions and was happy to endure their wrath as long as she got her way in the end. The period of Conservative government from 1979 to 1997 saw the increased centralisation of control over state education and the near obliteration of whatever degree of progressivism had managed to take hold in the 1960s and '70s. This trend was not reversed by New Labour when it held office from 1997 to 2010.

The belief that the best way to defend progressivism in education is to vote a left-wing party into government is, in my view, mistaken because left-wing parties are just as prone as right-wing ones to being eager to dance to the tune of a socially conservative tabloid media. What I am advocating instead is the replacement of the top-down model for running education with what I call the 'practitioner-led approach'. This is inspired by the Finnish model where what exists is a system based on high levels of teacher autonomy underpinned by high standards of training (see Pollari et al, 2018). I think, however, that such a system will only come about in the U.K. if teachers fight for it. Any kind of bottom-up movement is regarded here with deep suspicion by policy-makers, who believe that, in order to get their top-down reforms through, they have to take on and defeat the 'vested interests' who, motivated purely by self-interest, want only to block change.

What, specifically, do teachers need to fight against? In a word, *managerialism* (Enteman, 1993). In the 1990s, there was in the U.K. a revolution in how public services were delivered and the balance of power shifted away from professionals (teachers, nurses, doctors etc.) towards managers. This new elite of public sector managers attempted to apply pseudo-scientific techniques and strategies, which had originally been developed in the private sector, to the management of public services. For a managerialist, the only thing that matters is results, and ends justify means; if you can get people to do what you want by being open and honest with them, fine, but if you need to be deceptive and secretive, or to introduce stress-inducing levels of surveillance, that's also fine. In the education sector, the rise of managerialism went hand-in-hand with the disempowering of local education authorities. These LEAs had enjoyed the power to inject a philosophical dimension into the running of their schools, but they were pushed aside in favour of a model which required schools and colleges to be run as businesses. That is, they were forced to operate under a regime which required them to compete against each and be driven by performance targets. There are those who believe that this revolution has led to improvements across the public services, the chief beneficiaries being 'customers', who get more choice and a better service, and tax-payers, who get better value for money, but what has the price been in terms of loss of creativity, innovation and progressive thinking?

In an Orwellian twist, the word 'quality', for the managerialists, has acquired a new meaning. It now means the maintenance of detailed records by teachers for practically everything they do; if there is no paper trail, it is assumed not to have happened. The real goal here is *standardisation* – the extirpation of diversity in philosophical approaches. Is this really the same thing as quality? Fast food chains sell standardised products, but this does not mean that such products are of a high nutritional value. Standardisation in education has created a situation in which there is pressure on all teachers to conform to the same mediocre level.

Ideally, I would like to see a state of affairs in which practitioners doing the job on the ground were the ones determining the philosophical approach on which their work was based. Under such a state of affairs, managers at the level of the institution and policy-makers at the level of the system would be there simply to help teachers apply their respective philosophies by providing adequate funding, ensuring a safe environment, and offering constructive feedback on *technical* (as opposed to philosophical) aspects teaching practice.

The shock troops of managerialism on the ground are the 'authoritarian personalities'. The term was coined by Adorno (1950), who was interested in trying to discover why it was that some individuals developed fascistic, anti-democratic values while others did not. Using a research methodology based on questionnaires and interviews, he ultimately concluded that what made an individual susceptible to developing such values was their possession of a collection of certain personality traits:

- Rigid adherence to conventional beliefs about right and wrong

170

- Respect for legitimate authority

- Belief in aggression towards those who do not hold conventional beliefs or who are perceived to be 'different'

- A negative view of human nature, i.e. a belief that human beings are inherently selfish and dishonest

- A belief in simple solutions to complex social problems

- A tendency to scapegoat minority groups

- A preoccupation with violence and sexual morality

As if having to deal with authoritarians wasn't enough, we must also contend with the *narcissists*. These are people who try to manipulate situations so that everything revolves around them and the way they want things to be. If others submit to them, narcissists feign friendliness and admiration, but if anyone dares to say 'no' to them they are quick to drop the act and start throwing the toys out of the cot.

Many teachers feel that, in order to survive in their employing institution, particularly if it is a very conservative one, the best strategy they can follow is to accept the status quo and go along with something they don't really believe in for the sake of pragmatism. But this is to play into the hands of the authoritarians and narcissists. To waive the right to express your personal philosophy out of fear of not being accepted, or just for a quiet life, is something you may well live to regret; you could find oneself at the end of your career, having scaled the heights of the career ladder, nevertheless thinking to yourself, *"What the hell have I achieved?"*. When a person's drive towards self-actualisation through work gets frustrated, their motivation drops and they contribute less in terms of energy and commitment. They may even become ill because of it. A teacher somehow needs to find a way to prevent his spirit being crushed, to resist the pressure to become nothing more than part of the machine.

Milgram (1963) conducted a famous experiment on the tendency of human beings to obey instructions given by authority figures, even when obeying the instruction involves knowingly inflicting pain and distress on others. This, when one thinks about it, is the position a teacher is in when she is being instructed by people in authority to behave in a way she does not feel is in the best interests of her learners. In Milgram's experiment, unwitting subjects were instructed by a person in authority to deliver what they believed were ever-increasing levels of electric shock to an unseen victim. Two thirds of the subjects delivered the highest level of shock. This result is startling because it suggests that, for the majority of people, the distress caused by disobeying authority outweighs that of inflicting pain on others. But what of the one third who didn't keep obeying? Do some individuals possess a personality trait which allows them to resist the urge to obey authority?

Auzoult (2015) suggests that this trait is 'autonomy', i.e. the tendency of an individual to want to do things for herself rather than being instructed by others. If authoritarian personalities like both telling others what to do and being told what to do, autonomous personalities like deciding what to do for themselves and are relaxed about others doing the same. I would suggest that the teaching profession needs more autonomous personalities in its ranks, and that those teachers with autonomous personalities have a duty to be leaders in the workplace. By 'leaders', I do not mean in the sense of being promoted up the formal hierarchy into positions of authority over other teachers; those positions frequently go to people with authoritarian or narcissistic personalities. When I use the word 'leader', I mean in the sense of challenging people in authority, calling them account, critiquing them.

It is my contention that the way to combat both managerialism and the malign power of those with authoritarian and narcissistic personalities is for those who value professional autonomy to work to create a *counterculture*, and to make this the basis of a programme for change which can be pursued strategically. What does this mean in practice? Well, I am not advocating anything along the lines of Paris '68 or Tiananmen Square '89. I do not want to encourage teachers or learners to storm offices, occupy buildings and hoist the black flag of anarchism above their schools, colleges and universities. Like all forms of direct confrontationalism, this would be exhilarating to start with, but the inevitable defeat would take us back to square one, and the whole episode would make it easy to portray teachers as irresponsible and self-seeking.

I am advocating instead something much more sustainable. All teachers really need to do is draw and defend a line in the sand where one side is the realm of administration and the other that of professional autonomy. The teachers' side of this boundary would be a space where personal philosophies could be developed and experimented with without fear of interference from the other side. What should emerge is a sort *Bill of Rights* where the limits of the employer's control over the teacher are delineated clearly and unequivocally. It might be hoped that those who broadly agree with the views expressed in this book will form an influential minority within organisations where education is taking place and will be prepared to take a lead. But we must concede that, with the best will in the world on our part, those who either reject or are indifferent to our views are always going to be more numerous than us and it is always going to be a struggle for us to make our voices heard.

Most of the teachers I have worked with over the years are interested in politics only in so far as the top of the pyramid is concerned. Many of them will vote Labour because they feel that this is the party that will do most to support state education and protect teachers' terms and conditions, but are firmly apolitical where it comes to day-to-day workplace interactions. By taking this approach, they are implicitly accepting the right of managers to manage autocratically and the right of the organisation to impose its philosophy on teachers as opposed to allowing them to develop their own. I think that this is a naïve mindset that puts too much faith in the top-down model for achieving change. Admittedly, the national government has enormous power and vast resources at its disposal, but it would need to have the political will to make radical changes and, for that, the proposed changes would need to be popular with the electorate. In point of fact, the New Labour government of 1997 to 2010 was not without its successes in education policy. By targeting funding in the most deprived areas, they were able to close the attainment gap between middle class and working class school leavers. On the other hand, they were committed to league tables and testing, refused to reverse the trend towards increasing centralisation, and showed no interest in increasing teacher autonomy. If anything, they saw teachers as a barrier to the sorts of top-down reforms they wanted to impose.

We need to try to get the 'top-downists' to see that they are mistaken and throw their weight behind a different strategy, one of pushing for change from the bottom up. Some teachers might come to agree with this in principle, but then argue that the proper vehicle for radical bottom-up reform is trade unionism. In my experience, however, this belief is mistaken as the public sector unions' raison d'etre is to *resist* change, not to be its champion. The modern public sector trade union is typically a corporate entity, bureaucratic and hierarchical in its structure. Unlike in the private sector, where organisations need to adapt and change if they are to survive, public sector organisations grind on regardless and this has allowed workplace cultures obsessively resistant to change to take root and prevail in perpetuity. The unions are happy to play their part in protecting these cultures, but the irony is that it was the mentality behind such cultures that provoked the shift towards managerialism in the first place and continues to be used as an excuse for its continued existence.

When I became a union activist, my fundamental mistake was to misunderstand the reasons why teachers joined unions. Maslow (op. cit.) proposes that human beings have a 'hierarchy of needs', with basic physical needs like warmth and shelter at the bottom, emotional needs in the middle and the need for self-actualisation at the top. I had naively believed that teachers, as a group, were the sorts of people who had few worries in terms of their lower level needs and were thus primarily motivated by self-actualisation, i.e. applying their personal philosophies through their work in such a way that they made a difference to the lives of learners, thus fulfilling their own potential. There are some teachers who are at this level, but there are many more who occupy positions much further down Maslow's hierarchy and who consequently suffer from deep-seated feelings of fear, anxiety and paranoia. The thought of change amplifies these feelings and people who have them tend to join unions and look to them for help in resisting change. Because most union members have little interest in being actively involved in the running of the union, the elected officers and career officials tend to think of it as their own personal power base from which to pursue their own agenda, and to view the members as pawns in their power struggle. They will quite deliberately stoke up members' fears and insecurities so that they can present themselves as saviours. As long as they can successfully do this, their power base will always be there. For these reasons, working through the structures of a union might be *part* of an effective strategy to promote change – it's good to know they'll be in your corner if you need them – but it is unlikely to be sufficient on its own.

Sun Tzu, the Ancient Chinese military strategist, believed that there was no point in fighting unless you were practically certain you were going to win, and unless you were sure your objectives could not be achieved by other means. Not for him the headlong rush into glorious failure in the manner of the Charge of the Light Brigade; logic and cunning are more important than passion and courage. Successful wars are often waged and won subtly and quietly, in such a way that those against whom one is struggling do not even realise they are at war.

As I have said, I think that the key to cultural change is to create a counterculture. Being successful at this demands that we first understand the culture of which we are part. I have some observations to make about workplace culture:

- If you put a bunch of creative people together, everyone will raise their game to keep up with everyone else and wonderful achievements become possible.

- If you put a bunch of mediocre people together, they will simply muddle through in their own mediocre way, neither screwing up spectacularly nor achieving anything noteworthy.

- Whereas a creative person will tend to be happy in her own company, mediocre people like to form themselves into cliques. Such groups are a means through which mediocre people can wield collective power and get to feel important and special, and the solidarity amongst members is maintained through mutual hostility to outsiders.

- If you put a bunch of mediocre people together with a bunch of creative people and ask them to work together, as would be the case in most workplaces, this is where the fun and games start. The mediocre people will do everything they possibly can to drag the creative people down to their level so they are not shamed, and the creative people will do everything they possibly can to rise above this.

- If a decision taken from on high does not have the support of the workplace culture, the intention behind the decision will be subverted in the implementation process. This means that, if one has influence within the workplace culture, one wields enormous power, regardless of one's formal status.

Note: When I use the terms 'mediocre' and 'creative' here, I am not referring to innate characteristics but to *attitudes*. For instance, a person who is highly intellectually gifted might well have a mediocre, that is to say unimaginative and risk-avoidant, attitude to his work.

If we add to this powder keg naked ambition, status anxiety, and a liberal sprinkling of narcissistic and authoritarian personalities, what we end up with is an explosive cocktail of a workplace culture. Far from being blissful utopias based on harmonious co-operation, staff groups in educational institutions are typically living soap operas, rife with plotting and intrigue, with tearful psychodramas being played out daily. It is within this seething cauldron that a teacher aspiring to make a difference must learn to operate.

In any given workplace, one will tend to find that there exists an uneasy tension, just occasionally erupting into all-out war, with the rebels (creatives) in one faction and the conformists (mediocrities) in the other. We can thus talk in terms of the balance of power between the two groups. Creating a counterculture involves shifting this balance of power in favour of the rebels such that their perspective eventually becomes that of the mainstream and this in turn requires that we enter into and win what is sometimes referred to in the military as 'the battle for hearts and minds'.

In trying to win this battle, language and choice of terminology are of the utmost importance. For many teachers, terms like 'professional autonomy' and 'managerialism' represent abstract concepts which have little apparent relevance to the practical realities of their day-to-day working lives. Words like 'unfairness', 'bullying' and 'harassment', on the other hand, are highly emotive ones that everyone understands the meaning of. We need, therefore, to get colleagues to equate managerialism and authoritarianism with unfairness, bullying and harassment. This is what politicians call 'taking control of the agenda'. In this endeavour, unions are incredibly useful. Their officials have great experience in creating anti-bullying strategies and raising general awareness of bullying and harassment. In addition, union endorsement brings with it a certain legitimacy that makes people take notice. This might seem to contradict some of my previous comments about unions, but I make a distinction between members being subordinate to the agenda of officials and their use of the union as a vehicle for promoting their own agenda. It is a question of the dog wagging the tail rather than the other way round.

McGregor (1960) proposes two theories of employee motivation which he calls Theory X and Theory Y. In Theory X, employees work for *extrinsic* rewards, i.e. money. They do not enjoy their work for its own sake so they have to be manipulated into working by being offered rewards (carrot) and by being threatened with sanctions (stick). In Theory Y, by contrast, employees work not just for money but for *intrinsic* rewards such as self-expression and the desire to make a difference.

In my prison education department, Theory X was the implicit model managers worked with and there was an obsession with what teachers could and couldn't legally be forced to do under the terms of their contracts, as well as with counting the hours each teacher spent on the work premises. Theory X is inherently cynical, and cynicism on one side of the industrial relations divide tends to create cynicism on the other. Some of the teachers were as keen on sticking rigidly to the letter of the contract as the managers, and just as careful to count their hours. Whether a cynical management creates a cynical workforce or vice versa is a moot point – a chicken-and-egg debate.

I think that unions have to shoulder some of the blame for the preponderance of Theory X in education management. By focusing on material terms and conditions and by threatening to withdraw labour, they are implicitly endorsing the theory and this plays into the hands of the advocates autocratic management. Part of the problem here is that union activists and officials are often ardent disciples of Theory X. When I was a union rep, I remember a union official once declaring to a group of reps on a training course, *"Your job is to get the most amount of money possible for the least amount of work possible."* The truth is that managers and union officials are opposite sides of the same coin. The union official demands compliance from members just as the manager demands compliance from employees. They both have a vested interest in the system staying the way it is because they both owe their status and power to it.

Clearly, the belief that teachers should have a high degree of professional autonomy is based on Theory Y, and the belief in autocratic management on Theory X. Consequently, if we want to have a high degree of professional autonomy in our work places, we need to promote Theory Y as opposed Theory X in the attitude we show to our jobs. If we do this, and we combine such an approach with astute political tactics, we can push management towards a more democratic style of working. A manager does not want his job to be any harder than it needs to be and, from his point of view, it is much harder to apply Theory X than Theory Y. If he has a group of employees whom he can see behaving in accordance with Theory Y, why would he not go along with that? It is tactically counterproductive for teachers to confirm the negative stereotypes others have of them.

Strategically, the first task of the leader is to win the respect and confidence of a small group of like-minded individuals. This becomes the nucleus of what eventually evolves into a *subversive community*. She must try to get this group to look beyond the banal and the everyday and to *dream* – to imagine what might be and ask 'why not?'. The group then needs to collectively develop an inspiring vision of how things could be and an ability to communicate this in a way that motivates more people to join the group.

Bartolomé (2004), writing from her knowledge of the U.S. context, addresses the issue of educating would-be teachers in the ideological, as opposed to simply practical, aspects of being a teacher. She uses the term 'ideological clarity' to refer to the process by which teachers are brought to a deeper awareness of the socio-political context in which they work, encompassing an understanding of patterns of inequality based on ethnicity, gender and class, and proposes that such consciousness-raising should be an explicit part of teacher education. This would entail challenging the pro-establishment ideological baggage they carry with them when they enter the profession. Bartolomé concludes that it is indeed possible to bring critical pedagogical thinking into formal teacher training but, from my experience of the British context, I am not quite so optimistic. How realistic is it, after all, to expect the state to sponsor the long-term radicalization of the teaching profession and to have, as the establishment would see it, a steady stream of trouble-makers coming into our schools, colleges and universities? I would place more of an emphasis on teachers taking the initiative in expanding their own consciousness independently of formal structures, and on informal workplace leaders encouraging and guiding this process.

In trying to win other teachers over, it is good to catch them at the start of their careers if possible. When new teachers come into a workplace, they can be a breath of fresh air in that they have an uncorrupted way of looking at things and ask questions that fully enculturated teachers don't think to ask. Sadly, because people tend to desire acceptance, most of the new intake will sooner or later start to think and behave like everyone else. If, on the other hand, they can be engaged with in such a way that they start to realise that there is more than one way of being a teacher, and if they can be encouraged to persist with the reflective habits they developed in teacher training, and with the idealism that took them into teaching in the first place, they might yet be rescued.

The ideal workplace culture would be one where workers were always inspired to give of their all and be everything they possibly could be. Unfortunately, reality seldom reflects this. This is because human beings tend to carry with them all sorts of psychological baggage and this gets in the way of healthy relationships. Thus, people in groups can all too often bring out the worst in each other. Berne (1961) speaks of three psychological 'ego states' that any given individual can potentially occupy:

ADULT EGO STATE (the person is honest and genuine with other people).

PARENT EGO STATE (the person is either judgmental or paternalistic towards other people).

CHILD EGO STATE (the person has needy and dependent relationships with other people).

There are some individuals who are so stuck in either a child or parent ego state that they cannot change without some form of psychotherapy. Being a teacher has taught me, however, that there are some individuals who will behave like children if handled in an authoritarian manner, but who will become more adult if they are given autonomy. This, I think, is the key to changing the change-resisting mentality in the workplace – treat people like adults. The trouble, however, as we have seen, is that Theory X managers have a hard time believing that employees can be trusted with autonomy. A counterculture leader must therefore encourage colleagues to *assume* autonomy, thereby proving to doubtful managers that they can handle it, rather than waiting for it to be handed to them on a plate. Hence the crucial importance of being an example to follow. To use the phrase attributed to Gandhi, you should *"be the change you want to see in the world"*. By doing this, you develop a level of influence out of all proportion to your formal status. The following anecdote illustrates the point:

During my time in prison education, a new set of qualifications in maths and English known as 'Functional Skills' were introduced by the government. No-one in a formal position of authority in the department had made any effort to prepare for this, so I assumed responsibility without being asked, implicitly rejecting the 'not my job' mindset. I developed a system and made sure it ran smoothly, and the programme became a success. I was able, to some extent, to use the role to platform my personal philosophy. It was hard work, but it was rewarding and it meant that it was impossible for the employer to portray me as either unable or unwilling to take responsibility. I was thus able to demand a greater level of autonomy than would otherwise have been the case. My colleagues began to respect me as a leader and to listen to what I had to say. This was all part of my creating a narrative around myself as a leader and as someone to be taken seriously. As would-be initiators of a subversive counterculture, we need to do this; we need to become the authors of our own narratives. This is what successful political leaders do – they find a way to control the narrative surrounding them, as well as those surrounding their political opponents.

It is also important for the leader to communicate empathy and to avoid being judgmental. Criticising people will either provoke a hostile response or make them feel insecure and, when people feel insecure, they cling to the past as if it were a life raft and are happy to settle for mediocrity as long as things can stay the same. But, as we have seen in the context of getting learners to embrace risk, empathy and acceptance lead to a reduction in feelings of insecurity and a lowering of defences.

Counterculture leaders should tread confidently but cautiously. Managers don't like being got the better of by people below them in the hierarchy and we cannot afford to give them excuses to bully and harass us. Therefore, our own behaviour and work record need to be beyond reproach. In taking on people in authority, I would advise the following:

- Criticism should be of the idea, not the person; never stoop to personal abuse.

- Make it clear that what you are expressing is your *opinion* and nothing else. Do not make specific accusations unless you have evidence.

- To avoid being accused of bringing the employer into disrepute, do not distribute your views publicly, for example through social media or email. Private conversations with people you consider to be allies are a different matter, but make sure they really are your allies; you need to be certain that what you say isn't going to be reported to the wrong people and used against you.

- If you want to criticise a specific individual, as opposed to an idea or a policy, deal directly with the person you have the issue with; talk *with* them, not *about* them.

- Be logical and articulate rather than emotional; emotions escalate tensions.

- Whenever possible, re-frame the criticism of a thing as a positive assertion of its antithesis. For example, the statement, *"I don't like being micromanaged"* could be re-framed as, *"I prefer having the freedom to do things my own way."* The direct criticism thus becomes merely an implied criticism and is far less likely to provoke a negative response, although the meaning is still perfectly clear. We are not looking to make enemies or to hurt or humiliate anyone.

What we are trying to do in fact is build relationships with people in authority based on an adult-adult give-and-take ethos. Unfortunately, such a state of affairs is not easy to achieve in practice because, however adult you try to be, some people will stubbornly refuse to move from their child or parent ego state. In addition, many of the those who get promoted to positions of authority are consummately Machiavellian; that is how they get the promotions in the first place. For some of them, breaking their word is simply a tactic to be used whenever expedient. They have a mindset of ends justifying means and loyalty to their patrons above them in the hierarchy is the only thing that really matters to them. In dealing with these sorts of managers, we need to play hard ball. This means that we must get them to believe that a) they will not be allowed to get away with breaking their word, and b) we will follow through on whatever we say we are going to do. Whenever they give an assurance that they will do something, get them to commit to a deadline and make a written record. That way, if they fail to keep their word, a valid grievance will exist and it will be possible to threaten to make a formal complaint. If this approach is applied consistently, managers will eventually abandon the tactic of making promises they have no intention of keeping.

I once used this approach in a situation where a particular team leader was trying to micromanage me to the point where it became bullying. I went to see her superior, the department manager. The manager had no wish for the matter to escalate to a formal grievance as I had strong evidence of bullying, and a formal bullying complaint would have reflected badly on her as a manager. She was thus anxious to placate me. We agreed that the bullying team leader would be removed from having any authority over me and that the manager would make this clear to her. What the manager actually did was go to the team leader who had bullied me and ask her to go easy on me for a couple of weeks, but then quietly return to as things were – not what we had agreed! Things were fine for two weeks but then, sure enough, the team leader went back to bullying me as if nothing had happened. Instead of just resigning myself to this, as the manager and team leader presumably expected, I went back to the manager and reminded her of our original agreement. This time, I had the upper hand as the manager had been caught being in the wrong for breaking her word. The outcome was that the team leader was removed from having any authority over me and I was free to do my job however I saw fit. If you keep following through with relentless consistency on what you say you will do, over time you will build up a reputation as someone who means what they say and you will be treated with respect. Managers may not like you, but they will fear the consequences of crossing you.

A manager is an ordinary human being who has been fortunate enough to have been given an exceptional opportunity, not an exceptional human being whose superior status reflects the fact of this. It is incumbent upon them to behave with grace and humility when relating to those who have not been lucky enough to have had such an opportunity. They should also seek to use that opportunity to make their organisation better, both for its clients and for all who work in it, and they should be held to account over this. If professional teachers need a manager at all, they need a manager who is excited by the idea of bringing out the talent and leadership potential of everyone on their team. If teachers are not fortunate enough to have such a manager, they need to apply pressure to change her behaviour.

The person you have to primarily contend with if you want increase your personal power is the person one place above you in the hierarchy, the authority figure you interact with on a daily basis. If you are willing to take on this person, and if you are tough enough and astute enough to come out on top in an accumulation of daily micro-victories, you will have created a space for your professional autonomy to flourish. If we can get a great many teachers doing this, the cumulative effect will be a culture shift in the organisation itself.

Some employees will happily defend autocratic management, either because it relieves them of what they think is the burden of having to think for themselves, or because they are authoritarian personalities and it is an article of faith with them, or because autocratic workplaces offer opportunities for them to be promoted up the hierarchy. I believe, however, that autocratic management stifles personal growth, even for people who support it, and creates an environment in which bullying can flourish. In order to survive in such an environment, a person needs to suppress his natural impulse to express his individuality and, denied the opportunity to experience the joy of actualising his potential, he has to be content with patronising pats on the head: *"Well-done for doing as you're told."*

Teachers who fall into this kind of behaviour pattern remind me of the rats in BF Skinner's (op. cit.) operant conditioning experiments. In these experiments, rats in a box were trained to pull levers through a mechanism that released a food pellet every time they pulled the correct lever. Teachers subject to managerialist control techniques are in the same position as those rats; it is just that the food pellets in their case have been replaced by verbal praise, good observation reports and, for consistent obedience, promotions to the first rung of the management ladder.

Anxiety and depression have reached epidemic levels in affluent societies. Why is this? I have come to the conclusion that they stem from people feeling that they lack control over their own lives (in the case of anxiety), and from feeling that their lives lack meaning (in the case of depression). Before the medicalisation of happiness, people traditionally sought both these things in the concept of *community* and, for many, the most important of those communities was their workplace. A community is a place people feel they belong, where they can express themselves, where they feel valued, and where they have status. It is also, of course, a place where people take care of each other. But what if that sense of community is eroded through authoritarianism and managerialism? What if work becomes not much of a community at all, just a place of production where people are simply replaceable components in a machine, where what they are valued for is not what they think and feel as individuals in their own right but for compliance with instructions?

For many of us, rather than succumb to depression and anxiety, we find opportunities for being in control and for finding meaning inside our own minds. There, we discover our creativity and use it to make private worlds where we can find ourselves and be ourselves. If it just stopped there, it would be nothing more than self-indulgent escapism, but it doesn't have to stop there. If we can get enough people finding themselves inside their own minds, and if we can get enough of these people talking to each other, we can use this as a basis for re-making our workplaces as genuine communities. It requires, though, the all-out rejection of autocratic managerialism and the willingness to claim and defend autonomy. In so doing, each one of us becomes a leader, but a radically different type of leader from the conventional notion of what a leader is. This radical style of leadership is sometimes called *servant leadership* and its tenets were originally developed in an essay by Robert Greenleaf (1970).

Greenleaf's essay was written in response to a perceived leadership crisis in the U.S. (the time of the Vietnam War). He argued that only those organisations led by people with the highest regard for the people they were leading would survive in the future. Such servant leaders sees their role as helping others to grow as people, that is helping them to become healthier, freer, wiser, more autonomous, eventually evolving into servant leaders themselves. Such leaders react to problems by listening, not blaming, and listening in this context means deep listening – using imagination to get inside the skin of the speaker, to truly feel what it is like to be them. The servant leader avoids falling into the trap of interpreting what the speaker is saying through the prism of his own dogma, and is instead prepared to learn from her. Along with such deep listening should go an unconditional acceptance of the person for who they are. This should all sound familiar as it is exactly the same approach I advocated earlier in the book when I discussed teacher-learner relationships. If a leader can develop this kind of relationship with those he wishes to lead, they in turn will be more likely to listen to him and understand things through his frame of reference. Greenleaf does not claim that his philosophy of leadership is easy to pursue. On the contrary, it will inevitably involve setbacks and failures, but the leader should keep faith and persist. He should use experiences, both positive and negative, as opportunities to reflect on and refine his approach, not as an excuse to abandon it.

Greenleaf has little to say about authority because, in his view, a leader is defined by what she does and the sort of person she is, and this has nothing to do with whether or not she holds a formal position of authority. My own view is that, while there is nothing to prevent someone in a formal managerial role behaving as a servant leader, there is nothing to prevent a person on the lowest rung of the hierarchy being one either. When I was a learning support assistant, a pretty low status role in the college that employed me, I was, according to Greenleaf's definition, a leader – towards learners, towards other learning support assistants, and towards the teachers I was assisting. Leadership is building people up, not ordering them about, so formal authority is a superfluous quality. The antithesis to this – the obstruction or of another person's self-actualisation – is not leadership but oppression.

A criticism that some might be tempted to level against Greenleaf's concept of leadership is that its emphasis on individual development undermines teamwork; if everyone is set on expressing their individuality rather than showing disciplined loyalty to their superiors, so the argument might go, isn't this bound to lead to chaos? I disagree. In fact, I think that the reverse is true, that conflict arises when individual differences in outlook are unspoken, buried beneath the public espousal of unity. The differences will eventually find a way to bubble to the surface and erupt in the form of personal animosities. But if differences are expressed and discussed openly as they arise, and if there is a mutual willingness to listen and to allow others to be individuals, what happens is that people learn from, and grow to understand, each other. Conflicting points of view begin to move closer together until what develops is a synthesis based on consensus. This is what makes genuine teamwork possible.

Greenleaf was writing in an age of idealism, when progressive ideas were in the ascendency. I'm sure he believed at the time that his concept of leadership would shortly become the norm and that elitist and autocratic mentalities would soon fall into disuse. He could not have anticipated the severity of the conservative backlash. More than 50 years have passed since he published his essay, and yet autocratic management still thrives, given fresh impetus by managerialism and propped up by workplace cultures characterised by passivity and subservience. I believe that there are those within these workplaces who have the ability to take on the mantle of servant leadership and to consign autocratic management to the history books, but whether they will choose to do this or not is a different matter.

Charles Handy (1978) identifies four varieties of management culture in organisations. The first is the 'club culture', dominated by a single autocratic manager, in which an employee's status depends on how close he is to the autocrat. Such cultures are characterised by a great deal of interpersonal power politics as people compete against each other to gain access to the autocrat's inner circle. The second is the 'role culture', characterised by a clearly defined hierarchy and lots of rules and formal procedures. I have heard it described as a sort of democracy, although those at the bottom of the hierarchy don't usually get to vote for who they want at the top! The third is the 'task culture' in which hierarchies are downplayed and people work together to get tasks completed. Here, a person's status is determined neither by her formal job title nor by how close she is to the manager, but by the skills and expertise she brings to tasks. The fourth is the 'people culture', characterised by individuals doing their own thing with little regard for any notion of common goals. It is clear to me that, if we want to develop people and teams to their full potential, it is the task culture that we should be aiming to create.

But a task culture can only work if significant numbers of colleagues in a workplace believe in it enough to make it work. It requires great effort and a willingness to take responsibility, as well as a commitment on the part of each teacher to developing his own skills and expertise as much as he possibly can. This means accepting that one is going to be in a perpetual state of continuing professional development for the whole of one's career.

The reward is a feeling of *aliveness*, the knowledge that what one thinks, says and does has meaning, and the certainty that one is making a difference as an individual.

I believe that task cultures, and people cultures for that matter, are psychologically much healthier to work in than ones based on either charismatic personality cults or rigid hierarchies. One reason for this, as we have seen, is that, by allowing the employee greater freedom to express his individuality, they enable him to find greater meaning in his work. Another reason is that, when we eliminate the need for employees to *compete* against one another, either to get closer to the manager's inner circle or to win a promotion up the career ladder, the employee can afford to focus all of her energies on self-development and on being creative.

Workplace cultures can change, but there needs to be a critical mass of leaders present to bring the change about. My prison education department had a strong club culture. The lack of willingness on behalf of too many teachers to show leadership allowed the manager to build around her a small clique composed of herself and a handful of loyal sycophants, and it was this clique that dominated decision-making. As a consequence, the clique's groupthink ensured that the department failed to respond creatively to challenges posed by a changing financial environment (government cuts were biting hard). It began haemorrhaging money at an alarming rate, yet still not enough leaders came forward to take responsibility. In the end, the manager and most of her clique were either demoted or made redundant, and this ushered in a new era of increased authoritarianism. At the time, I thought that the old club had got exactly what it deserved, but on reflection I see that the people truly to blame were those teachers who failed to show leadership, the ones who said, *"That's not my job."*

Chapter 10

Education for Happiness

There are, it seems to me, too sorts of unhappiness. The first sort results from a lack of basic necessities like food and shelter – being stuck at the bottom of Maslow's hierarchy of needs. There are plenty of people in this position even in affluent countries such as the U.K. Then there is the other sort, the unhappiness experienced by people who have material possessions in abundance but still feel that something is lacking. They are reasonably high up Maslow's hierarchy but just can't quite seem to get any higher. This sort of unhappiness is connected to a sense of emptiness and of being disconnected from one's true nature, to a feeling that one's life lacks meaning and purpose. An individual afflicted with this sort of unhappiness – let's call it *alienation* – might react to it in various ways. For instance, they might construe it as a medical problem and consult a psychiatrist. The doctor might diagnose 'free-floating anxiety with mild depression' and prescribe a drug such as Prozac. Another way of trying to deal with the problem might be to use consumerism to drown out the unhappiness, to fill the emptiness with commodities, what the humanist-Marxist philosopher Herbert Marcuse (1964) called 'commodity fetishism'. Apart from the fact that such a behaviour pattern will not cure the underlying unhappiness, the ceaseless yearning for cheap consumer products leads to worker exploitation and environmental degradation, things which both cause and exacerbate the first kind of unhappiness.

The cure for both sorts of unhappiness is *consciousness* – consciousness of the hidden structures and mechanisms which are the root cause of the unhappiness. In the case of alienation, the unconscious factors are repressed instincts, whose energies, through the process of sublimation, become redirected into an insatiable longing for material goods. In the case of the kind of unhappiness that comes from economic deprivation, the unconscious factors are the deep workings of an economic system which keeps the poor poor and the rich rich. Education, in the most complete sense of the word, needs to promote consciousness in both the psychological and the political spheres, that is to be both inward-looking and outward-looking.

The word 'counterculture' was used by the cultural historian Theodore Roszak (1968) as an umbrella term to describe a number of radical social, cultural and political movements, which collectively had the potential to transform western society for the better. Unfortunately, this potential was never truly fulfilled and what followed in the 1970s and '80s was a conservative cultural backlash . So, what went wrong? My view is that the movement lost its way in no small part because most working class young people, without the benefit of having had a high quality education, found the various ideas associated with the counterculture bizarre and bewildering. Consequently, they did not feel it was for them and showed no interest in joining in. I feel that we are in a comparable moment in the first half of the 21st century in that a potential exists to create a powerful countercultural movement, broadly humanistic and environmentalist in character. However, this potential can only be realised if the state education system becomes an engine driving a revolution in consciousness.

In recent times, the dream of economic affluence, particularly home ownership based on easy access to mortgages, has been used as a means of securing social stability; if someone is working hard to pay off a long-term mortgage and maintain an affluent lifestyle, not just for themselves but for their families, they are inevitably less inclined to put their jobs at risk by rebelling against the social order. This dream, however, has a nightmarish side in that it is built on massive economic inequality and a catastrophic level of environmental destruction. Moreover, western governments have in recent years increasingly struggled to meet the material aspirations of younger people, particularly with regard to home ownership. This has created a generation gap and is fuelling a general sense of dissatisfaction amongst the young.

The present generation of younger people, the first in modern times to be materially worse off than their parents, are surely fertile ground for the cultivation of countercultural consciousness. If they come to believe that they have little realistic prospect of achieving the consumerist dream, perhaps they could be persuaded to reject it altogether and experiment with something else? It might be possible to get them to see their inability to find an opportunity to become part of it as a lucky escape from what it inevitably turns them into. The zombie movies of George A. Romero – *Night of the Living Dead* (1968), *Dawn of the Dead* (1978) and *Day of the Dead* (1985) – are biting satires on consumerism. In these films, reanimated corpses roam the land, their only motivation being to *consume* (in their case, the flesh of the living). Beyond this, they are to all intents and purposes dead. Someone needs to ask young people whether this is really what they want out of life.

Some kind of cultural revolution is long overdue and education, as a primary shaper of values, is well-placed to play a central role in this. The key, I believe, is for teachers to see themselves as facilitating a process in which learners reflect deeply on what they want out of life and develop alternative value systems upon which to build more authentic, more fulfilling lives than the dream of material affluence could ever provide them with. Thus, the school, the college and the university stop being part of the problem and start to become part of the solution.

The cultural rebellion of the '60s had a conflict between generations at its centre. Roszak suggests that older radicals at the time saw the youth counterculture as frivolous and decadent, and for this reason were careful to distance themselves from it. Perhaps they feared it, or perhaps they just didn't understand it. At any rate, they missed the opportunity to guide and shape it. History does not have to repeat itself. The task of getting learners to question mainstream values within the formal educational context is undeniably a challenging one because the system itself encourages a treadmill mentality and a competitive ethos. Few dare to point out the absurdity of this, and the ones who do are not taken seriously. It is simply taken for granted that what young people want, what they *should* want, is to live lives very similar to those of their parents and that it is the function of the state to ensure that they get this.

The task before teachers is one of encouraging learners to re-direct their feelings of dissatisfaction away from the usual scapegoats (racial and ethnic minorities and foreign governments) and towards the dominant culture itself. This can be achieved by creating emotionally safe classrooms where controversial ideas can be openly discussed and strong feelings expressed. It needs to begin early in a child's education – as early as possible. Far from being Marxist, what I am proposing is a radical form of humanist individualism in which everyone is deemed capable of constructing and implementing his own authentic version of 'the good life'. There is no prescribed correct choice here, only the correct choice for the individual. For some, this will simply be a re-affirmation the values of the dominant culture, but others may create radical alternatives.

For Roszak, the driving force of the '60s counterculture was not a desire to re-distribute wealth but to resist increasing alienation. But, whereas for his Marxist contemporaries such alienation was a direct consequence of the capitalist economic system, Roszak believed it to be a consequence of the ever-growing tyranny of what he termed the *technocracy* – an all-powerful elite of experts and their political allies manifesting an obsessive desire to control and exploit. This technocracy wields its power mostly through making itself seem natural, normal and inevitable. No socialist revolution, argues Roszak, could ever change this reality; the technocracy is as much a feature of state-owned economies as it is of capitalist ones. The only thing that *can* change it is a revolution in consciousness.

The word 'intellectual' is often used to denote a person who prefers thought to action, the abstract to the practical. For that reason, teachers can be reluctant to identify with the word. But the Marxist theorist Antonio Gramsci (1948), himself imprisoned by Mussolini's Fascist state, uses it in a more politicised sense. For him, ideas and culture are the means by which systems of oppression secure the consent of the oppressed. They do this by presenting the existing political and economic structures as serving the interests of the people as a whole. The people are made to believe that they just have to remain obedient and placid, and believe in the experts, and all will be well in the end. To perpetuate this lie, a certain type of intellectual is required, one who propagates ideas which legitimize the system. Counteracting this, however, there is another type of intellectual, one who takes on the role of pointing out the unfairness and destructiveness built into the system and encourages its victims to question it. This is the role that teachers are well-placed to play.

We need a conception of the teacher as *provocateur*, helping to mould a generation of young people who themselves go on to become provocateurs, championing both the individual human being and the natural environment in response to the destructive power of the technocracy. This is a conception of the teacher diametrically at odds with that of the teacher as technician following orders, teacher as administrator of tests, teacher whose sole function is to competently train a new generation of technicians to competently serve the technocracy.

A teacher with strong emotional intelligence is in a good position to help curb the darker excesses of youthful idealism, to provide balance and a more nuanced perspective. By sensitively channelling anger and frustration into constructive activity, they can rein in any slide towards hatred and the justification of violence. The classroom could become a place where serious issues are discussed, but in a playful and humorous way. Too much earnestness can get out of hand and lead people down all sorts of destructive and self-destructive paths. We have a template for such a scenario in the fictional character of Holden Caulfield in J.D. Salinger's *The Catcher in the Rye* (1951), though there are countless real-life examples. But the most dangerous course of action for teachers to take would be to ignore the needs of young people to use the classroom as a forum for discussing issues they feel passionate about. This would be to push them into the clutches of extremist groups under whose influence they could be radicalised without the protection of a voice of reason urging them to respect the humanity of those they happen to disagree with.

Another way in which young people try to escape feelings of alienation is by experimenting with drugs and immersing themselves in the subcultures that surround them. In the '60s, those involved in the counterculture might well have enthused about the benefits of taking 'mind expanding' substances, but hindsight allows us to see the naivety of this attitude. I am willing to entertain the notion that, for an individual who has been on a sincere journey of self-exploration for many years, the next step in that process might be to use psychedelics to go yet deeper into her unconscious psyche, and then use what she finds there to aid her creativity. However, most people who experiment with drugs are trying to escape reality rather than to understand it more deeply, to make themselves *less* conscious rather than more so. For such people, their relationship to the drug is another form of commodity fetishism – a fake kind of joy used as a substitute for the real thing. How can education help to get them away from this? Well, we need to somehow flip young people's perception of education so that they see it not as something that reinforces feelings of alienation, but as an antidote to it. This demands that we start to break down walls – between the intellectual and the emotional, between the conscious and the unconscious, between 'them' and 'us'.

Within this context, learners need to be free to explore different identities, to re-invent themselves as many times as they like. Teachers can inspire this by bringing art, music and other creative forms into the classroom – the more provocative the better. It is likely that, for some young people, this is the only kind of formal education they are willing to engage with. The alternative would be exclusion and the bleak dead end of a future to which this leads.

When discussing values with learners, the aim should always be to get them to think for themselves, never forcing them to take up positions, and the teacher must resist the temptation to fill silences with his own beliefs. He may of course offer observations, throw in questions, or provide factual information if it is relevant, but he must not seek to control or censor the flow of thoughts. He does need to ensure that all voices are heard, to do all he can to get learners to understand that there is never one single 'truth', but many 'truths' compatible with the available evidence and that the right to express one's own truth goes hand-in-hand with developing the sensitivity to accept the truths of others.

In dealing with groups of learners, a teacher should be aiming to create micro-communities, where each member is sensitive to the needs of every other member. This ideal state of affairs needs to be worked towards patiently, and there will inevitably be conflict along the way. This should not be mistaken for 'disruption' or 'challenging behaviour' that needs to be suppressed, but as a natural part of healthy group development. Tuckman (1965) sums up this process in four words: 'form', 'norm', 'storm' and 'perform'. In the 'form' and 'norm' stages, the group members come together and get to know each other. 'Storm' describes the tricky intermediate stage, characterised by drama and emotion, where conflicts need to be worked through. If this stage is negotiated successfully, the group finally reaches the 'perform' stage in which members are able to work creatively together. One of the things I like about Tuckman's model is that it fits nicely with Bion's theory of group dynamics; we see a journey from a state of high anxiety manifested through conflict to one of low anxiety manifested through creative collaboration .

Teachers and learners are together quite capable of creating learning environments, whether physical or virtual, for themselves without the help of managers or administrators. Such people can be useful as an efficient means of getting funds and resources to where they need to be but, ultimately, it is managers who need teachers and learners to justify their existence, not the other way round. Once teachers and learners realise this – that the emperor is not wearing any clothes – managerial mystique collapses and managers become servants rather than masters.

I am sure that there will eventually come a time when we have machines with artificial intelligence that can 'teach' in the most narrow, soulless sense, and it will be technically possible to create institutions where human teachers will be there just to operate the machinery. Learners would be placed not in classrooms, where they could build relationships with other learners, but in sealed-off booths following their own individualised learning programmes derived from diagnostic assessments, themselves administered by computer. How joyless! How depressing! How alien to human nature! Teachers need to do what they can to prevent this becoming the dominant mode of the delivery of education in the future.

One of the most radical philosophers of education ever to come to public prominence was Ivan Illich. In his book *Deschooling Society* (1971), he depicted the traditional school as a quasi-industrial factory system where learning, rather than being a natural part of human experience, was a commodity to be acquired, amassed and consumed. Perhaps his most startling assertion was that schools made people stupid. This statement struck me as absurd when I first read it, but deeper reflection led me to realise that there was something in it. Let's take as an example an area of education of which I have direct personal experience – adult basic education:

Initial assessment tests are used to label certain individuals as having problems with either literacy, numeracy or verbal communication. They are then given 'diagnostic' tests to further ascertain the specific nature of their inadequacy. Note the word itself – *diagnostic*. It is all about labelling a person as defective. If someone is made to *look* stupid and *feel* stupid then he is surely made to *be* stupid. Doing this on a massive scale has spawned a whole industry providing employment for (mostly middle class) professionals hired to help the (mostly working class) 'deficient' people. Formal institutional education also renders people stupid by encouraging them to regard all the 1knowledge they have accrued outside of the system – in informal settings where they have learnt things in practical contexts – as worthless and as needing to be forgotten and replaced with the kind of formalised knowledge the system provides them with.

Illich believed that this sort of counter-productive lunacy could be replaced by a system of voluntary networking, what he called 'conviviality', in which any given individual wishing to learn a particular subject or skill could connect with a person able and willing to teach it. The school or college would simply be the physical location where teachers and learners met up and agreed privately between them how to proceed, not hierarchical institutions where teacher-learner interactions were constrained by an all-powerful managerial 'them'. I accept that this is a fantasy at the current time, but what if we were to behave *as if* it were true? What if we treated learners *as if* they were people with whom we had made a private agreement to teach and, to facilitate this, we had simply hired a classroom? Taking such an attitude and pushing the concept as far as we possibly could before we started to get resistance from management would radically change the whole dynamic of the teacher-student relationship. It would allow learners to say to the teacher, *"This is what we want to learn; could you please teach us it?"*, instead of the teacher saying to the learners, *"This is the curriculum; this is what you're required to learn."* Who knows where this experiment may lead.

Chapter 11

Interview with the Learner

In this chapter, I am presenting a transcript of an interview with a learner, together with a commentary, because I think it highlights some of the major themes of the book.

Maddy was 24 years old at the time of the interview. She was a former student at the adult education institution Ruskin College, in Oxford, where she had completed an Access to Higher Education course (social sciences) a couple of years earlier. Coincidentally, I had taught at this college myself so I was well-acquainted with its culture, although our times there did not overlap. On the strength of her Access certificate, Maddy had been offered a place on the BSc Psychology course at Solent University (Southampton). She had taken up the offer but dropped out before completing her first year. Apparently, the excessively protective environment she had enjoyed at Ruskin had left her ill-prepared for the rigours of university. I was helping her develop study skills in preparation for another attempt at higher education. She is dyslexic and suffers from both anxiety and self-esteem issues, and I suspect that the three things inter-react in a variety of ways. It would be fair, I think, to say that Maddy would not include the ability to perform formal deductive reasoning tasks as amongst her greatest strengths, and she's not brilliant at memorising long lists of facts and figures. She does, however, have a natural warmth and an exceptional capacity for building relationships with others – what could be called high emotional intelligence. She is also highly curious and throws herself into learning with an enthusiasm the like of which I have rarely come across. She is thus a joy to teach.

Simon: What were you saying about what you wanted me to help you with?

Maddy: So, I would like you to help me with how to write a written essay.

Simon: How to write a written essay?

Maddy: Yes.

Simon: Was that not one of the things you were supposed to learn when you did your Access course at Ruskin?

Maddy: Well, that's the thing. When I was at Ruskin there were many things I began to learn, but one of them wasn't actually how to structure an essay.

Simon: Right.

Maddy: With the college, I found it more as, you know, you go there, you go to your lesson, and if you don't get your work done on time they pressure you. And, when they pressure you, you know, you feel you have to do things in a certain time. And if you don't, they kind of say, "Okay, pass it to me and I'll do your work for you". And they do the work for you.

Simon: Really, they do the work for you?

Maddy: Yes.

Simon: So, did you get anything out of your time at Ruskin do you think?

Maddy: Erm, well ……

Simon: You got a certificate I suppose.

Maddy: Well, I did my Level 2 qualification in social sciences and then I did my Level 3, you know equivalent to A-level, in social sciences. And I got my certificate for it, but, erm ..... I think I can be honest with you, I don't feel that I learnt much. When I went to university, there was nothing I could bring from college to do my Level 4 course. And I believe also that the only thing that Ruskin taught me was how to get work done fast in a short period of time.

Simon: So, when you went to university, that wasn't really much use to you. Is that what you're saying?

Maddy: Yeah, because the thing with the university is they won't help you with your work. They won't do something for you which is ..... you know, you should do it yourself anyway because you won't learn that way. They give you all the material – books, and websites. Whereas Ruskin, they didn't do that. They didn't say, "This is the book you should read." Not once. They never said, "This is the materials." They never really gave a website. They just said, "This is what's on a website, and this is what we expect, and this is the due in time for your essay. And, if they think people are less kind of smart than others, then they'll say, "We'll meet one-to-one." And, during that time one-to-one, they'll have done the essay for them.

Simon: Really? It's like as if, almost what you're saying is that what they cared most about was getting as many students as possible to the end of the course without failing.

Maddy: Yeah. Er ….. I'll tell you what it was about. It was about Ruskin having a high succeed level, and about Ruskin being known as students that come from a background which involves crime, broken homes, mental health issues being able to, you know, take on courses and being able to pass. They knew that some of the students were vulnerable and I think they took a part of playing that and thought, "You know what? These people that are going through deep major stuff." Because everyone had a lot, you know, the majority of students, about 85 per cent, had mental health issues there. They knew that, if they just did the work and stuff it would be less stress for them and they would get higher ratings and markings from different colleges.

Simon: I see. Yeah, I think I understand what you're saying. So what made you decide to go to Ruskin in the first place then?

Maddy: Well, one thing I did like about Ruskin was they give you a chance, they give you an opportunity, and most colleges don't do that. I mean, for an Access course you don't have to have any qualifications and unfortunately I didn't have any qualifications.

Simon: Yeah. So, sounds like that, er ….. it wasn't all that successful at school. Would that be fair?

Maddy: Yeah, school wasn't really my best, you know ….. er ….. the best time of my life, you know. I got bullied.

214

Simon: You got bullied? Right.

Maddy: Yeah.

Simon: Why do you think you got bullied?

Maddy: Erm ….. I wasn't the popular girl, the most prettiest ….. erm, you know.

Simon: So who was doing the bullying, then? Was it other girls, or …..?

Maddy: Yeah, no, boys also.

Simon: Girls and boys?

Maddy: More boys.

Simon: More boys? *(note of surprise in voice).* What do you think would make them want to bully you?

Maddy: Well, I think it was just the immaturity of the age, the showing off. It wasn't just me, it was other people. It was quite a bit ….. it was because I had eczema around my lips at that time, so they used to take the mick out of my eczema. And I used to have it round my face. And it was really visible. You know, you could see it. It was when I used to come into lessons they would say, you know, "dried lips", or "crusty", and I used to put so much cream on, but it wouldn't go away.

Simon: So, you got bullied over your appearance?

Maddy: Yeah.

Simon: How did that make you feel?

Maddy: I didn't go to class because of it.

Simon: So, you skipped school you're saying?

Maddy: Yeah, most of my English lessons. And science. Whenever that boy was there.

Simon: Oh, right. And did you tell anybody about it?

Maddy: My dad.

Simon: You just told your dad? And did your dad tell the school?

Maddy: Well, I didn't want him to because it would cause big issues. But afterwards, it was all right. It was okay. I just came to terms with it.

Simon: So, was there no-one on the staff at the school that you felt close enough to to be able to talk to about it?

Maddy: The thing is with schools, as well, back in my time, they don't care. They don't, you know, they don't really care as much as they put out that they do. And, you know, they say they're here for help, and they do this and that, but when it actually comes to it they don't do nothing. I mean, I reported an incident before where I've been bullied from a guy. They said, "Oh, that's not good." And they didn't exclude him, they didn't ….. they maybe had a little word, but what's that gonna do? They don't really care.

Simon: No. So, taking the bullying issue out of it, did you like school or was it …..?

Maddy: It was all right. I liked college more.

Simon: You liked college more? Why do you think that was?

Maddy: Because, with college you're kind of with grown-ups, and with Ruskin I tended to be with different people, different ages, and they tended to be more older, whereas school you're with people that, you know, are much younger and ….. school's a bit of a mess-about time and, you know, nobody really likes school anyway to be honest.

Simon: Why do you think a lot of kids don't really like school?

Maddy: Erm, I feel like kids don't like school because it's a place where people kind of tell you what to do, and I don't think people like to be told what to do, and especially young, you know, teenagers, because that's what we were. I mean, we were, you know, under 18 at the time and, erm, I feel like ….. as I said again, the bullying. A lot of bullying happened in schools that people are not aware about, and it can cause mental health issues. And, you know, the other reasons is some people just don't like to wake up early, and they don't like a routine in life. Some people want to just get a job and they don't really like education and they find it boring, so ..... .

Simon: Do you think if school had been a bit different, a bit more relaxed, you might have enjoyed it a bit more? What do you think?

Maddy: Erm..... you know, the thing is with school is ..... you know ..... you either love it or you hate it. I feel like there isn't really an in-between, and for me I didn't enjoy it. But I think like maybe if school wasn't so taught on education and more on self-love and more about mental health, I think that would be better because I feel like, you know, like all these years of self-education but no self-love or self-care, you know, it ..... what has it really taught us?

Simon: Yeah *(pause)*. What do you do think helps you to learn, then. How do you best learn when you're trying to learn something new, say? What's the best way to go about doing it, for you?

Maddy: So, for me it's visual.

Simon: You're a visual learner?

Maddy: I'm a visual learner. So, I like to look at pictures and diagrams. Erm, I like to cut up cards and, you know, draw things on so I can remember it by. I feel like, for me, I like to pick something that's bright and colourful so it makes me enjoy learning more. Whereas, if you're reading a power point with a hundred lines it kind of ….. erm ….. it kind of bores you off. You know, with education I think it needs to be more fun and more creative, and you know, you need to put it in a way where you enjoy it, because you can't really enjoy something if you're forced to learn because that way it's not going to stay in the brain.

Simon: Right, so you don't like it when someone tries to force you to learn something? You want to have more freedom to do things your own way? I'm sort of putting it in my words, so ….. .

Maddy: Yeah.

Simon: Yeah? So you like have the freedom to kind of just organise your learning in the way that works for you?

Maddy: Yeah.

Simon: And you tend to draw pictures, do you, when you're learning?

Maddy: Yeah, I draw pictures in a notebook, or I like to look at books with pictures and less writing. I feel like that way I learn better and that way it stays in my brain.

Simon: Good. Now, you told me once that you had dyslexia?

Maddy: Yeah.

Simon: When did you find out that you had dyslexia?

Maddy: So, this is actually a really interesting topic to talk about because I actually found out I had dyslexia four years ago.

Simon: Yeah?

Maddy: So, erm, I was actually at a college before Ruskin College – Oxford City College.

Simon: Okay, I know it, yeah.

Maddy: Yeah, so I did a few tests and I filled in a lot of, erm, paperwork, and I did a computer assessment. And it turned out that I was dyslexia. I had dyslexia, sorry. And I wasn't that shocked because, you know, my teacher kind of said to me, "You know, Maddy, when you're kind of, when you read and stuff out in the class I can see that you're taking quite a long time." And, erm, you know, she asked me a few questions like, "How does it look to you?", and I described to her and everything. And then, erm, she said, "I'm a bit concerned because you kind of muddle up your words in like a written poem, and all this other stuff." So, it did kind of knock me down a bit because I did feel a bit different, but I've got ways of helping me.

Simon: Good, so how do you compensate for your dyslexia, then, when you're in a learning situation? What do you do to help you overcome your dyslexia?

Maddy: Well, I just ….. basically, I, like I said, I learn in my own way and my own technique.

Simon: So, pictures. You've already talked about pictures.

Maddy: Yeah.

Simon: So, making pictures.

Maddy: Yeah.

Simon: Okay, good, and when you were at Ruskin, did *they* give you help because of your dyslexia?

Maddy: No.

Simon: So, nothing other than ….. you said earlier that sometimes they'd do the work for you to try to get you through.

Maddy: *(Laughing)* Yeah.

Simon: Did they give you any help with actually learning itself, with the learning process, because of your dyslexia?

Maddy: No.

Simon: So nothing in that field, okay.

Maddy: No.

Simon: Okay, let's think now about leaving formal education and going into work. So, what jobs have you done since you finished school?

Maddy: That I've done ….. are you talking about, like, work?

Simon: Yeah, any kind of work, whether it's paid or unpaid, part-time or full-time.

Maddy: So, I've done a lot of retail I'll say.

Simon: Retail work?

Maddy: Yeah, just clothing stores and …..er …..er …..and caring work.

Simon: And care work. Yes, good. Do you think that your education in any way prepared you for that? Did the education that you got at Ruskin, or Oxford City College or at school, did it help you in your work life?

Maddy: Yeah, it did.

Simon: In what ways?

Maddy: Because, in your work you're like you'll always have to calculate or make notes, and obviously maths taught me how to calculate and learning

English taught me how to write notes, you know, spelling mistakes and all of that stuff.

Simon: What about in a work situation where something unexpected happened, where there was a problem and you needed to solve it, for example you had an angry customer who hadn't got what they wanted?

Maddy: No, I don't think education helped with that.

Simon: So how would you cope with those situations, then? Say you've got an angry customer who wants to make a complaint because they don't feel they've been given good service. How would you cope with that?

Maddy: I think the best way is just to reassure them that, you know, there's always an option that I can offer them and, you know, give them different types of *(pause for thought)* strategies they want to take. So, if I said to them, "Would you like me to do this for you?", or, "Do you want me to get you that?" Calm them down.

Simon: Sounds good. Did you have to teach yourself how to do that or did someone help you?

Maddy: No, I had to teach myself.

Simon: So it's kind of like you learnt how to do it through experience?

Maddy: Yeah.

Simon: Okay, good. Well-done! *(pause).* Okay then, what would you say would be your greatest strengths? What are your greatest strengths as a person?

Maddy: Ah, this is a hard question, honestly! Let's see ….. erm ….. don't know what to say to this one.

Simon: What are you really good at?

Maddy: I feel like I'm really good at ….. erm ….. I'll probably say ….. erm ….. sorry, just got a few things *(laughs).*

Simon: Go on. It could be anything.

Maddy: Yeah ….. erm.

Simon: So you were just saying about when you were in retail.

Maddy: Yeah, I'm good reacting calmly to, you know, bad situations, and I'd say my strength is I've got patience.

Simon: Is that patience in dealing with other people, do you think?

Maddy: Yeah, and, er, just in the work environment, because I, with me, I've ….. I've done a lot of work with care, and it was honestly it was very, very hard. You know, I would do 12-hour shifts and I would start from 7.00am and finish for the evening, and it would require a lot of work to do, you know. I would say I was very determined. When I want something, I won't stop until I get it.

Simon: That sounds like a really good quality to have. So you're a very patient person, you're very patient. It sounds like from the work you've done that you've got quite good people skills. Would that be fair?

Maddy: Yeah, that's it. I've got good people skills. Yeah, I'm really good at communicating with people. I've got quite a bubbly personality. So I think I can mix that very well wherever I go to social events, to work events, to meeting new people, and home life, and I can bring all of that to my different aspects of life where I am. So, that's something to have because, for some people, they, some people are just ..... you know, I'm not saying there's anything wrong with not being bubbly but I feel some people are just, you know, they like to keep themselves a bit quiet, or they don't like to attract as much.

Simon: So, given that that's probably your biggest talent, then, do you think that your education helped you to develop that talent in any way?

Maddy: Yeah, because when I was doing education, erm, I remember one time when I was at college, and it was Ruskin, erm, they did say to me actually, I was close to giving up, and they did encourage me not to leave the course, and they said to me, "Now think about how good you'll feel when it's done, you know, when you've got the certificate." And there were times when I had breakdowns, you know, "I can't do this." And it's really hard, you now I don't understand certain things. Erm, one lady kept pushing me and pushing me. She worked in the office. She wasn't actually my teacher, she actually just worked in the office. I had a good relationship with her.

Simon: So, that one person encouraged you to believe in yourself?

Maddy: Yeah. She used to email me to come in, she used to phone me where am I. I mean, you know, "Make sure you get in class." Stuff like that.

Simon: Okay, and do you think if it wasn't for her you might have dropped out, or ….. ?

Maddy: Yeah, yeah.

Simon: So, what did she say to you, then, to make you not drop out and keep going? Is there anything specifically that she said to you?

Maddy: *(Laughing)* She said she could see I've got a bright future.

Simon: Good, good, good, okay *(pause)*. Right, so sometimes in the past you've talked to me about your anxiety. Do you think that your experiences in education have helped with that, or have they made it worse, or ….. what's the relationship between your education experiences and your anxiety?

Maddy: Erm, I don't feel that it has helped much, no. I feel like, like I said, school should have taught you about self-love and, you know, how important our mental health is rather than, "This is this, that is that." You know. No, I felt that I taught that myself. While I was getting older, I found out for myself how to manage with my anxiety.

Simon: How old were you when you could say, "I suffer from anxiety?", when you realised that you had it?

Maddy: 17.

Simon: 17? So, you were probably just leaving school at that time.

Maddy: Yeah.

Simon: Ok, and how does your anxiety link to your self-image, how you see yourself and how you think other people see you?

Maddy: I mean, it changes on different days. Some days it can be really bad and some days it can be really good. Erm, you know sometimes I try not to think about what other people think about me, or about how much I think about myself because that can put you in a really dark place. So it's best to sometimes just ignore the world and put your headphones in and just focus on what's important.

Simon: Okay, yeah. And how encouraging have your family and friends been in your education?

Maddy: Yeah, my friends have been really, really encouraging and really proud because I went to university, and, you know, I studied psychology. I feel that that was a huge step, especially from being at school with no qualifications, and then getting to college, and then doing my A-levels which was very intense because it was three A-Levels in one and you had to do that in seven months. So you had such a short period of time doing, you know, hard subjects. And, you know, I passed it, I did it, so that for me was a huge achievement because I actually went to university, erm, about seven years later than I actually should have.

Simon: Yeah, yeah. So, your family, your friends and your community, and your culture, that was all encouraging?

Maddy: Yeah.

Simon: Okay, good. We'll stop there then.

Maddy: Okay.

Simon: Well-done. Thank you.

Maddy: Was that ok? I didn't go on, did I?

Simon: No.

The first thing to be said about the interview is that it was in itself a learning experience for Maddy. With all the hesitations and stumblings over words left in the transcript, we get a real sense of someone being in the moment, reflecting as she went along and thinking out loud rather than coming out with pre-rehearsed statements based on what she thought I wanted to hear. She was, in the process of composing a story about herself, experimenting with her self-concept, exploring the possibilities for the future by reflecting on the past. On reading back over the transcript, it occurred to me that I had not asked her why she had left Oxford City College, the institution she'd attended before going to Ruskin. When I did ask her about it, at a later date, she said that she had been doing a course in social care but had decided not to finish it because *it wasn't for her*. What a wonderful example of a person tearing up one version of who she was and reconstructing herself from the fragments!

The conversation was a real learning experience for both of us which was only possible because Maddy and I had invested time and effort in developing a high quality teacher-learner relationship based on empathy, acceptance and genuineness, and where we felt totally relaxed with each other. There was more than a hint of transference/counter-transference in the relationship.

It is interesting that I had to prompt her to talk about her greatest strength – her people skills. It was as if she had never thought about it in terms of being a strength, that she felt I was judging her solely according to her academic skills, and it was her sense of insecurity in this sphere that I think was behind some of her self-esteem issues. You might assume that most teachers would regard the identification and nurturing of talent as central to their role, but it doesn't seem as if anyone within the world of formal education had ever really tried to make her feel special because of her people skills; perhaps the nearest she ever got to that was the encouragement she got from the administrator at Ruskin!

Maddy's description of the incident where the teacher did an assignment for her rang true with me. Behind this, I feel, is a deep collective discomfort with the idea of failure amongst the staff at that institution. I have every sympathy for the teacher to whom Maddy referred; the cultural pressure to do whatever it took to ensure that every student succeeded was immense there, and realism in this regard was something the management seemed to have little interest in. They were much more concerned about their brand image and market niche as a college that supported 'vulnerable learners'. The underlying problem, I believe, was managerialism, in particular the replacement of an authentic philosophy and ethos with an 'ends justify means' mentality.

The same problem had existed in the prison education department at HMP Bullingdon, where I had worked prior to going to Ruskin. There, external examinations, which should have been conducted under strict exam conditions, were administered in classrooms with no time limits and, in some cases, someone sitting next to the candidate prompting them through the questions. This is clearly a form of corruption, and I personally took a lead in putting a stop to it, but it again illustrates the consequences of the replacement of integrity with the amoral cynicism that is such a strong feature of managerialist workplace cultures.

In addition to rampant managerialism, the other aspect of the cheating problem is the low expectations teachers have of learners; at both Bullingdon and Ruskin there appeared to be little faith in what learners were capable of achieving on their own merits and I think that this attitude was unconsciously transmitted to the learners themselves. To overcome this problem, there needs to be a cultural shift away from understanding the learner in terms of her deficiencies, and on trying to compensate for them by fair means or foul, towards understanding her more in terms of strengths, and looking to give her opportunities to develop them. Maddy undoubtedly has her vulnerabilities, but she also has numerous strengths. Why not develop a learning programme for her that foregrounds these strengths whilst keeping awareness of her vulnerabilities in the background?

Of course, a cynic might take the view that there are certain people in society who just do not have the innate ability required for genuine academic achievement and that the best we can do for them is to give them the illusion of success and allow them to live in a fantasy world. Well, the problem with this is that, eventually, the walls surrounding the fantasy will crumble and the individual will be exposed to reality, ill-equipped to deal with it.

Other than give them the illusion of success, what other, more authentic, ways might a teacher have of dealing with a struggling learner? One way would be to encourage perseverance – tell them to take the failure on the chin and to keep trying until they succeed. If they want to succeed badly enough, they'll go along with this, but there is another way. Remember Maddy's reply when I asked her why she left Oxford City College: *"It wasn't for me."* For a learner to decide that a programme of learning isn't for them is not the same thing as quitting because of lack of perseverance. It is, on the contrary, a moment of self-awareness, of facing up to reality. Maybe she could have succeeded, if she had worked incredibly hard, if she had kept going in the face of all the inevitable setbacks, if she had made use of all the help legitimately available to her. But would it have been worth it? Some learners might ultimately decide that it would be better for them to devote their energies to things that give them joy rather than slogging away at something they find soul-destroying. It is their choice – a seizing of control – and we should respect it as such.

Turning now the bullying issues Maddy alluded to, her experience of bullying at school may have contributed to the development of her ongoing anxiety and self-esteem issues, especially her insecurities over her appearance. Sadly, bullying seems to be a common feature of all closed hierarchical institutions such as schools, prisons and the armed forces. A bully is someone who feels powerful when he makes another person unhappy and will latch onto anything about that person that makes her different. I believe that a lot of bullying can be explained as displacement behaviour. The pattern goes something like this:

An individual feels angry towards someone with power over him. Perhaps this person has humiliated him in some way, made him feel weak. He wants to get back at this person but he cannot because the person is too powerful. So he looks for someone else to hurt, someone less powerful than him. This makes him feel better about himself, restores his self-esteem, but at the expense of damaging someone else's. The question is, if this kind of behaviour pattern is endemic to the culture of the institution, how can it be eliminated?

Maddy herself offers a clue to solving this problem when she talks about the need for schools to teach pupils more about what she calls 'self-love'. Maddy uses this phrase as a synonym for good mental health and what I think she is driving at is the need, as she perceives it, for the education system to concern itself not just with the development of cognitive skills but with psychological well-being and with helping learners to work on developing strong and healthy self-concepts. This would allow pupils who were feeling unhappy to talk about their feelings openly and, through that process, learn ways of dealing with them that were better than inflicting pain, either on self or others. What we are talking about here is *preventative* mental health care. By creating a healthy emotional environment, i.e. one of empathy, genuineness and acceptance, we remove the initial causes of bullying. This could begin at a very early age; I touched on this idea in Chapter 3 when I discussed the use of stories to address emotional issues.

I think that Maddy is absolutely right when she says of school that you either love it or you hate it. We would both put ourselves in the category of those who hated it, citing lack of regard for mental health as significant factors in our hatred. In her case, the problem was the lack of opportunity to talk about mental health in the school environment. With me, it was more about the anxiety-inducing effects of authoritarianism and the lack of acceptance of me as an individual. Both Maddy and I carry the psychological scars of our experiences.

'School phobia', in which a child experiences so much anxiety at the thought of going to school that she is literally unable to attend, is a well-known phenomenon. However, in seeking to understand it, we tend to fall into the trap of viewing the situation through the lens of a 'medical model', where the problem is seen as being located in the child. According to this model, the child who refuses to attend school is suffering from a psychological disorder such as 'separation anxiety' or 'social anxiety'. Once the correct diagnosis has been made by an expert, a course of treatment can be prescribed. Note the number of medical terms used: 'disorder', diagnosis', 'treatment', 'prescribed'. We need to get away from this way of thinking and start viewing things through the lens of a 'social model' in which is the school, not the child, that is the problem.

Going back to Maddy's 'you either love it or you hate it' line, I think that the ones who hate it are like the one third of subjects in Milgram's social conformity experiment (see Chapter 9); there is something inside them which resists the pressure to conform. This thing is not a defect that needs to be extirpated, but a precious gift that needs to be celebrated and nurtured. It is by attempting to suppress it that we induce the anxiety and strengthen the resistance. Pupils in this situation remind me of Harry Palmer, the character played by Michael Caine in the film *The Ipcress File* (dir. Sidney Furie, 1965, and based on the 1962 novel of the same name by Len Deighton). Caine plays the part of Harry Palmer, a secret agent who resists the brainwashing power of the sinister Ipcress machine by repeating his own name over and over again and by deliberately inflicting pain on himself. It is as if he needs to continually remind himself that he exists and that he has his own unique identity. The acronym 'Ipcress', incidentally, stands for 'Induction of Psychoneurosis by Conditioned Reflex under Stress', and the machine itself is a brilliant metaphor for the technocracy, of which the state schooling system is a significant part.

Conclusion

The nature of creativity is such that it is sometimes only in retrospect that we fully understand why we did things the way we did and what it all really meant. Even then, we can never be entirely certain that our conscious interpretations truly reflect our unconscious intentions. In this final section, I will offer some tentative thoughts concerning what it's all been about, but it is also up to you, the readers, to draw your own conclusions.

I wrote much of this book at the time of the 2020/21 coronavirus pandemic and it was inevitable that this wider context would influence me to some extent. To my understanding, a virus replicates itself by infiltrating individual cells of the host organism and hijacking the system by which they replicate themselves. In other words, it uses a bottom-up strategy. I think that cultural change in organisations happens in kind of the same way. That is, a new perspective establishes itself at the level of individual consciousness and then tries to take control of the whole organisation bit by bit by getting itself transmitted from person to person. Like a virus, it is subject to natural selection and, in trying to get round the organisation's defences, it will mutate and acquire modifications, eventually evolving into a variant uniquely adapted to survive in that particular environment. In getting this book 'out there', I imagine myself to be the first person in the transmission chain for the ideas it tries to convey.

Our state education system needs new ideas so that it can let go of the ones that no longer work and rebuild itself from the bottom up. One of the most pernicious of these obsolete ideas is that the function of the system is to identify each learner's level of natural ability and to prepare them for a role in life reflective of that ability level. The consequence of failing to let go of this idea is that the system continues to reinforce long-standing patterns of social inequality. If we could consign this mentality to the history books, that would leave space for a different paradigm to take root and flourish. This new paradigm would be based on the assumtion that the purpose of education was to develop the creative potential of each and every learner, and that a person's capacity to be creative was not constrained by their level of inherited intelligence. Moreover, there would be a secondary assumtion that fear and anxiety were counterproductive to the development of creative potential and that empathy, genuineness and acceptance were the conditions most conducive to it.

If we wait for this paradigm shift to be led from the top, we will be waiting forever, like Vladimir and Estragon in Samuel Becket's play *Waiting for Godot* (1953). What is needed instead is for teachers to take responsibility and lead a reform movement from the bottom up. This requires them to reframe the very notion of what it means to be a teacher, to expand, deepen and politicise the way they think. They need to stop making excuses for inaction and start to act.

I believe that the teaching profession now more than ever has a pivotal role to play in creating a society that is fairer and more compassionate. In the days when working class people were employed in large numbers in heavy industries, the nature of the work itself created solidarity. This led to radical consciousness which translated into political power. But we live in a very different world now, one where the working class is much more fragmented and whose interactions are likely to be characterised as much by competition as co-operation. Solidarity is consequently much more difficult to achieve in the workforce and this is why we now need to look towards education rather than organised labour as the most viable route to radical consciousness.

Historically, radical movements have come and gone. The British version of 1960s counterculture ('The Swinging '60s') was truly astonishing in the way it spawned a dazzling explosion of creativity in so many different fields. However, it was a counterculture doomed to eventually run out of steam and yield to a conservative backlash. This was in part because it was ultimately elitist, a story about a highly privileged few getting the opportunity to escape their working class roots and fulfil their creative potential, with little benefit to those left behind, a point elegently made by Sandbrook (2015). These few may have been talented, and they may have worked hard, but they were also *lucky* – lucky because they benefitted from an implicit belief in both natural inequality and in the idea that only the most able deserved the best opportunities. The Punk movement, which came along a few years later, was less elitist and more overtly anti-establishment, but lacked leadership and ended up being commodified and swallowed up by consumerism before it had had a chance to mature. I would hope that, if we were going to revive the idea of counterculture for the 21st century, state school teachers would take a leading role in the movement, a movement which aimed both to make society fairer and to develop the creative potential of all of its individual members.

I said in the Introduction that we understand the world, and our place in it, through stories, and this has been a theme running through the whole book. Stories are floating around us all the time, moulding our thoughts, behaviours and feelings without our necessarily being aware of it. Take the story of Covid-19. The standard narrative was that a blameless human population was unfairly victimised by a cruel disease. But there is another version of that story that should also be told. In the non-standard version, the blameless victim was the planet and the human race the disease. The virus was the planet's attempt to fight back, its immune response so to speak. This illustrates why I love stories so much – they are capable of being re-told and flipped around in all sorts of different ways so as to convey all sorts of different meanings. When a person can master this skill, when she can re-tell the stories around her in such a way that she has complete control over who she is and what her life means, she can truly be said to be empowered. This is what education, in the truest sense of the word, can achieved.

239

References

Abraham, G.Y. 'Critical Pedagogy: Origin, Action & Consequences.' KAPET, 2014, Vol. 10.

Adorno, T. W. (1950). The Authoritarian personality. New York: Harper.

Auzoult, L. 'Autonomy and Resistance to Authority', Swiss Journal of Psychology, 74(1), 2015, 49-53.

Awan M.A. (2017). 'Freudian Notion of Psychoanalysis: Its Implications in Contemporary Teaching Practices.' Advances in Language and Literature Studies. Volume 8, Issue 5.

Bachkirova, T. (2011). Developmental Coaching: Working with the Self. Maidenhead. O.U. Press.

Bandler, R., Grinder, J., & Andreas, S. (1979). Frogs into Princes: Neuro Linguistic Programming. Moab, Utah. Real People Press.

Bartolomé, L.I. 'Critical Pedagogy and Teacher Education: Radicalizing Prospective Teachers'. Teacher Education Quarterly, Winter 2004, p.97-122.

Bergson, Henri (1911) An Essay on the Meaning of the Comic. London. Macmillan.

Berne, E. (1961). Transactional Analysis in Psychotherapy: A Systematic Individual and Social Psychiatry. New York. Grove Press.

Bettelheim, B. (1976). The uses of enchantment: The meaning and importance of fairy tales. New York: Knopf : distributed by Random House.

Bion, W. R. (1961). Experiences in Groups and Other Papers. London. Tavistock Publications.

Boyd, L. (2015, November 14). *Neuroplasticity: After Watching This, Your Brain Will Not Be the Same Again*. TED Talk video. Accessed on YouTube (29/03/2020). https://www.youtube.com/watch?v=LNHBMFCzznE&t=15s

Britzman, D.P. (2013). 'What gives between psychoanalysis and education?'. Journal of the American Association for the Advancement of Curriculum Studies, Volume 9.

Brookfield, S. (1998) 'Critically Reflective Practice', The Journal of Continuing Education in the Health professions, Volume 18, p.197.

Bruner, J. S. (1960). The process of education. Cambridge, Massachusetts. Harvard University. Press.

Buzan, T., Buzan, B. (1993). The Mind Map Book. Essex, England. Pearson Education Group.

Cain, S. (2012). Quiet: The Power of Introverts in a World That Can't Stop Talking. New York. Random House.

Campbell, M.B. 'Biological Alchemy and the Films of David Cronenberg'. In Grant (ed.) (2004). Planks of Reason. Lanham, MD. Scarecrow Press.

Claxton, G. (1997). Hare Brain, Tortoise Mind: Why Intelligence Increases When You Think Less. London. Fourth Estate.

Conrad, J. (1997) Heart of Darkness. New York. Signet Classics. First published 1899.

Cox, C.B. and Dyson, A.E. (1971). The Black Papers on Education. London. Davis-Poynter.

Csikszentmihalyi, M. (1990). Flow: The Psychology of Optimal Experience. New York. Harper & Row.

De Bono, E. (1970). Lateral Thinking: A Textbook of Creativity. London. Ward Lock Educational.

Dewey, J. (2011). Democracy and Education. Milton Keynes. Simoom & Brown. (First published 1916).

Ellis, A. (1984). Rational-Emotive Therapy. In R.J. Corsini (Ed.). Current Psychotherapies (3rd ed.). Itasca, II. Peacock Press.

Enteman, W.F. (1993) Managerialism: The Emergence of a New Ideology. Madison, Wisconsin. The University of Wisconsin Press.

Erickson, Milton H. (1983). Healing in Hypnosis: The Seminars, Workshops, and Lectures of Milton H. Erickson. Volume I. (Ernest L. Rossi, Margaret O. Ryan, & Florence A. Sharp, Eds.). New York. Irvington.

Foucault, M. (1975). Discipline and Punish – The Birth of the Prison (1975). New York. Vintage Books.

Frankl, V. E. (1984). Man's Search for Meaning. An Introduction to Logotherapy. New York. Simon & Schuster. First published 1946.

Freire, P. (1970). Pedagogy of the Oppressed. New York: Continuum International Publishing Group.

Freire, P. (1974). Education for Critical Consciousness. New York: Continuum International Publishing Group.

Freire, P. (1998). Pedagogy of Freedom: Ethics, Democracy and Civic Courage. New York: Continuum International Publishing Group.

Fromm, E. (1942). The Fear of Freedom. London. Routledge & Kegan Paul.

Freud, A. (1937). The Ego and the Mechanisms of Defence. London. Pub. by L. and Virginia Woolf at the Hogarth Press, and the Institute of psycho-analysis.

Gardner, H. (1983). Frames of Mind: The Theory of Multiple Intelligences. New York. Basic Books.

Gazzaniga, M.S. (1970). The Bisected Brain. New York. Appleton-Century Crofts.

Gazzaniga, M.S. (2005). 'Forty-five years of split brain research and still going strong'. Nature Reviews Neuroscience Vol. 6, pp. 652-659.

Gladwell, M. (2008). Outliers: The Story of Success. New York. Little, brown and Company.

Goleman, D. (1995). Emotional Intelligence: Why It Can Matter More Than IQ. New York. Bantam Books.

Good, Thomas L. (1987). 'Two Decades of Research on Teacher Expectations: Findings and Future Directions'. Journal of Teacher Education 38: 32, pp. 32-47.

Gramsci, Antonio, 1891-1937. (1971). Selections from the Prison Notebooks of Antonio Gramsci. New York. International Publishers. First published 1948.

Greenleaf, Robert K. (1970). The Servant As Leader. Cambridge, Mass. Center for Applied Studies.

Greer, G. (1971). The Female Eunuch. New York. McGraw-Hill.

Handy, C. B. (1995). Gods of Management: The changing work of Organizations. New York: Oxford University Press. Originally published 1978.

Harris, T. A. (1969). I'm OK, you're OK: A practical guide to transactional analysis. New York. Harper & Row.

Hebb, D. (1949). The Organisation of Behaviour: A Neuropsychological Theory. New York. Wiley.

Hines, B. (1969). A Kestrel for a Knave. London. Penguin.

Illich, I. (1983). Deschooling Society. New York. Harper Colophon. First published 1971.

Iverson, A, Pedersen, A Krogh, L and Jensen, A (2015), Learning, Leading and Letting Go of Control: Learner-Led Approaches in Education, SAGE Open, October-December 2015: 1-11.

Janis, I. L. (1972). Victims of Groupthink: A Psychological Study of Foreign-Policy Decisions and Fiascos. Boston. Houghton Mifflin. Chicago.

Jung, C.G. (1923). Psychological Types, or The Psychology of Individuation. London. Paul, Trench, Trubner.

Kellaway, L. (2021). 'What is the Point of Schools?'. Published in the weekend edition of the Financial Times on 06/03/2021.

Kelly, G. A. (1955). The Psychology of Personal Constructs: Vol 1 and 2. New York: WW Norton.

Koffka, K. (1935). Principles of Gestalt psychology. San Diego, CA. Harcourt Brace.

Köhler, W. (1929). Gestalt Psychology. New York. Liveright.

Kruger, J. and Dunning, G. (1999), 'Unskilled and Unaware of it: How difficulties in recognising one's own incompetence lead to inflated self-assessments'. Journal of Personality and Social Psychology, 77(6) pp.1121-1134.

Laing, R.D. (1960) The Divided Self: An Existential Study in Sanity and Madness. Harmondsworth. Penguin.

243

Marcuse, Herbert, 1898-1979 (1964) One Dimensional Man; Studies in the Ideology of Advanced Industrial Society. Boston. Beacon Press.

Maslow, A. H. (1970). Motivation and Personality. New York. Harper & Row.

McGregor, D.M. (1960). The Human Side of Enterprise. New York. McGraw-Hill.

Meltzer, D. (1992). The Claustrum. London. Karnac Books.

Milgram, S. (1963). Behavioral Study of Obedience. The Journal of Abnormal and Social Psychology, 67(4), 371–378.

Neil, A.S. (1960). Summerhill: A Radical Approach to Child-Rearing. Oxford. Hart Publishing.

Obama, B. (1995). Dreams From My Father. New York. Random House.

Obama, M. (2018). Becoming. New York. Crown.

Ough, Tom. (28/09/2018). 'Ade Adepitan: "The faster I was, the stronger I was, the more independent I became." ' Retrieved from The Telegraph website (30/05/2020) https://www.telegraph.co.uk/men/thinking-man/ade-adepitan-faster-stronger-independent-became/

Piaget, J. (1936). Origins of Intelligence in the Child. London. Routledge and Kagan Paul.

Pinker, S. (1999). How the Mind Works. New York. Norton & Company.

Pollari, Pirjo; Salo, Olli-Pekka; and Koski, Kirsti. (2018). In Teachers We Trust – the Finnish Way to Teach and Learn.i.e.: inquiry in education: Vol. 10: Iss. 1, Article 4. Retrieved from: https://digitalcommons.nl.edu/ie/vol10/iss1/4

Robinson, K., & Aronica, L. (2016). Creative Schools: The Grassroots Revolution that's Transforming Education. New York. Penguin Books.

Rogers, C. R. (1983). Freedom to learn for the 80's. Columbus, Ohio. C.E. Merrill Pub. Co. First published 1969.

Rogers, C.R. (1961). On Becoming a Person. Boston. Houghton Mifflin.

Rosenthal, R., & Jacobson, L. (1968). Pygmalion in the Classroom: Teacher Expectation and Pupils' Intellectual development. New York. Holt, Rinehart and Winston.

Roszak, T. (1968). The Making of a Counterculture. Berkeley and Los Angeles. University of California Press.

Salinger, J. D. (1991, c1946) The. Catcher In The Rye. Boston. Little, Brown And Company.

Sandbrook, D. (2015) The Great British Dream Factory. London. Penguin.

Sartre, Jean-Paul (1943). Being and Nothingness: an Essay on Phenomenological Ontology. Reprint, London. Methuen & co, 1972.

Skinner, B. F. (1938). The Behavior of Organisms: An Experimental Analysis. New York. Appleton-Century-Crofts.

Steele, T. and Taylor, R. 'Marxism and Adult Education in Britain', Policy Futures in Education, Volume 2, Numbers 3 & 4, 2004.

Stenhouse, L. (1975). An Introduction to Curriculum Research and Development. London. Heinemann.

Sun Tzu (2000). The Art of War. Translated by Giles, L. (1910). Leicester. Allandale Online Publishing.

Syed, M. (2015). Blackbox Thinking: The Surprising truth About Success. London. John Murray.

Tuckman, Bruce W. (1965) 'Developmental sequence in small groups', Psychological Bulletin, 63, 384-399.

Tyler, R. W. (1949). Basic Principles of Curriculum and Instruction. Chicago. University of Chicago Press.

Vygotsky, L. S. (1978). *Mind in society: The development of higher psychological processes* (A. R. Luria, M. Lopez-Morillas & M. Cole [with J. V. Wertsch], Trans.) Cambridge, Mass.: Harvard University Press. (Original work [ca. 1930-1934]).

Weale, S. (2019, September 20). *'Shameful rise': 18% of children now leave school as low achievers*. Retrieved from The Guardian website 05/04/2020.
https://www.theguardian.com/education/2019/sep/20/shameful-rise-18-of-children-leave-school-without-basic-qualifications

Wertheimer, M. (1959). Productive Thinking. New York. Harper.

Winnicott, D. W. (1953). Transitional objects and transitional phenomena; a study of the first not-me possession. The International Journal of Psychoanalysis, 34, 89–97.

Yerkes, R. M., & Dodson, J. D. (1908). The relation of strength of stimulus to rapidity of habit-formation. Journal of Comparative Neurology and Psychology, 18(5), 459–482.

Yousafzai, M. & Lamb, C. (2013). I am Malala: The Girl Who Stood Up for Education and Was Shot By the Taliban. London. Weidenfeld & Nicolson.